"A BEAN STALKER'S INSIGHTS . . . LIVELY STUFF . . . A DELICIOUS LATE FALL READ."
—*Boston Globe*

"*BEAN* IS A BEAUT . . . HILARIOUS AND INFORMATIVE."—*Sports Illustrated*

"FUNFILLED . . . ABOUT AN INTRIGUING CHARACTER who developed an equally intriguing business . . . The reader gets the full flavor of an unusual American institution."
—*Newark Star-Ledger*

"MYTH, HISTORY AND GOOD READING . . . amusing and written in a lively manner . . . illuminates the world out of which that well-known catalog comes."—*The Christian Science Monitor*

M. R. MONTGOMERY is a columnist for the *Boston Globe*. After graduating from Stanford University, he and his wife, Florence, came to Massachusetts, where they have been irregular, but fundamentally loyal, customers of L. L. Bean.

In Search of
L.L.Bean
M.R. Montgomery

Drawings by Mary F. Rhinelander

A MENTOR BOOK

NEW AMERICAN LIBRARY

NEW YORK AND SCARBOROUGH, ONTARIO

MENTOR TRADEMARK REG.U.S. PAT. OFF. AND FOREIGN COUNTRIES
REGISTERED TRADEMARK—MARCA REGISTRADA
HECHO EN CHICAGO,U.S.A.

SIGNET, SIGNET CLASSIC, MENTOR, ONYX, PLUME, MERIDIAN
and NAL BOOKS are published *in the United States* by NAL PENGUIN
INC., 1633 Broadway, New York, New York 10019, *in Canada* by The New
American Library of Canada Limited, 81 Mack Avenue, Scarborough,
Ontario M1L 1M8

First Mentor Printing, November, 1987

1 2 3 4 5 6 7 8 9

PRINTED IN THE UNITED STATES OF AMERICA

For Florence,
who stands beside me, dreaming.

Contents

CONTENTS

Bought me a pair of cowhide boots, to be prepared for winter walks. . . . I feel like an armed man now. The man who has bought his boots feels like him who has got in his winter's wood. There they stand beside me in the chamber, expectant, dreaming of far woods. . . .

Henry David Thoreau
Journals December 3, 1856

In Search of
L. L. Bean

THE first L. L. Bean product I saw was a pair of Maine Hunting Shoes, size 8 narrow. They belonged to my father, but were regarded as a sort of second-class family heirloom for a quite separate reason. The cover of the first *Life* magazine was photographed by a Miss Margaret Bourke-White while wearing those selfsame boots, as Miss Bourke-White had arrived in Fort Peck, Montana, unprepared for the local mud. If my father had larger feet, the boots would have had no special significance at all.

The boots disappeared, possibly into a church yard sale, and it was twenty years before I saw another pair. This second pair was walking across Harvard Square, and, in an odd coincidence, on the feet of a person with a large camera strung across his shoulder. This person was also wearing a pair of cotton khaki pants, a button-down-collar shirt that poked up through a Shetland wool crew-neck sweater, and a tweed jacket. It was a Preppie, the very first one I ever saw in full dress uniform.

Like everyone who moves to New England, I eventually

3

had to make the pilgrimage to Maine for fall foliage and a visit to the Bean factory store. This was twenty years ago, before they put carpeting on the stairs, before L. L. Bean died, before the small company in Freeport, Maine, became a mail-order giant.

Maine, the state on which the whole mystique of L. L. Bean rests, is indelibly inscribed on the minds of all persons who managed to sneak in a childhood before television, and a few who survived the magic box with their ability to read intact. The only purely European-American mythological figure, excepting the Native American myths to which we have only recently begun to pay attention, is the saga of that Maine lumberjack, Paul Bunyan, and his blue ox, Babe. He ended up in Minnesota, but heroes end up many places, it is where they come from that matters, and Bunyan forever made Maine a place of big trees and winters so cold that they froze the very words as you spoke them and the birds' songs also, and the dogs' barkings — and the noise in the spring was awful.

But Maine is not the cultural possession of the whole nation. Although we are all aware of it, and have some sense of it, it is, and has been for four generations, the particular habitat of the Natives, and people from Boston, New Haven, New York, and Philadelphia. These people, who can roughly be described as Easterners, as opposed to people from Maine, who are called Down-Easterners by people who aren't, are the visitors who have always been the primary patrons of Maine, and of L. L. Bean, Inc. Their descendants, their wide-flung relatives, and, most particularly, their *imitators* are the second great cadre of Bean customers.

So, this is a book about Maine, the Eastern sporting establishment, and L. L. Bean, in no particular order. They are inseparable, historically, and maintaining the illusion that they are inseparable today is the major marketing problem facing L. L. Bean, Inc., as it passes into the era of modern management and annual sales of $235 million, a hundred times the business that the Old Man did in his best year. So we must talk of Maine Hunting Shoes and shipping docks and skiing wax as well as Atlantic salmon, black flies, the big woods, float planes, and back roads — for it is all an inseparable weave. There is no L. L. Bean without Maine, and, as you will see, there may be no Maine without L. L. Bean, the state's best advertisement.

In the course of making inquiries toward the construction of this book, I had occasion to speak with the public relations (they like to call it public information, but let us be honest about it) person at the Maine Department of Inland Fisheries and Wildlife. I needed some historical information about hunting regulations in the state of Maine, and he wondered why, and I told him. "Well," he said, "another piece about the mystique of L. L. Bean, is it?" Mr. Shoener of Fish and Wildlife can not only pronounce "mystique," but inject a certain cynicism into the word, drawing out the second syllable a little longer than is necessary.

I hope it is not entirely sizzle and no bacon. It should be a book about the reality, and the mystique, in that order. It is, of course, only my idea of the reality, and not L. L. Bean's idea, nor that of their president, Leon A. Gorman, grandson of the founder. That is because this is a most unauthorized biography of the company. L. L. Bean likes publicity, but they would, understandably, like to control the flow, the quantity, and the content, of the publicity.

A few years ago (December 1981) I wrote a lengthy story on the company for the *Boston Globe Sunday Magazine*, and that led to the agreement between the publisher, and myself, to expand on the subject in book form. When I informed executives at L. L. Bean that the article they said they liked so much was about to become the size of a Blue Ox, they demurred, writing, among other things, that "Our customers see the Company as having a certain 'mystique' that will be difficult to maintain as more and more information about the Company is reported to the public." The letter went on to note that Bean's itself, in conjunction with a New York publisher, was about to emit two books, an *L. L. Bean Guide to the Outdoors*, and the *L. L. Bean Fish and Game Cookbook*, and thought a third book with the name L. L. Bean in the title would detract from their projects. In addition, someday soon, there will be a company-sponsored biography of L.L. and his company, under the personal direction of Leon A. Gorman. So be it. Even if they feel the pressure dropping down on them, I simply assume that anybody who puts 28 million catalogs in the public mail every year is open to public comment, and this book is it.

There is, of course, a third consideration which makes the Company, as they capitalize it, unwilling to be subject to great public scrutiny. It is entirely privately held, at this writing, by heirs of L. L. Bean, and it is difficult to be rich in this most parlous age of panhandlers, bunkum artists, obscene phone callers, Internal Revenue agents, and assorted non-shoe persons. There appears to be no taste for L.L.'s style, one of constant, cheerful, self-promotion, within the family today. I have, basically, heeded their request not "to come up sneaking around Freeport."

In spite of the company's objection to being laid out like an unetherized patient on the table, they have continued to be quite generous with information that is public, if not widely distributed. For several years, beginning in 1975, the year that truly modern business management arrived at L. L. Bean, the company has cooperated with the Harvard Business School case study program — and there is nearly as much financial data available on the company as would be available if it were publicly held and required to file audited statements with the Securities and Exchange Commission. Considerable recent financial information in this book thus appears courtesy of the President and Fellows of Harvard College, and the Baker Library of HBS.

The cases, in addition to financial data, give a fairly clear picture of the means by which Bean's has grown so astonishingly. And there is no reason to expect that the company will change substantially, so far as the way it does mail-order business, in the foreseeable future. The pattern has been established. The only way it will change is, perhaps, if the company should become publicly held, or sold, like so many mail-order businesses, to one of America's conglomerates. Something will have to be done, sooner or later, to liquidate the assets of the family shareholders — the inevitability of death and taxes is not just an aphorism, but a prime force that may eventually move the company to some form of public ownership, either independently, or as a subsidiary of another publicly owned corporation. But that is in the future. The subject of this book is not the problem of inheritance taxes, but how something as insignificant as a pair of rubber-bottomed, leather-topped boots should create an institution large enough to attract the attention of taxmen, corporate suitors, and other predators.

A last word. I have, like many a resident of greater Boston, depended on the state of Maine as a last refuge, in time of trouble, from the reality of traffic, burglar alarms in the night, work-weeks, heat, dirty snow, and rivers the color of the great, gray, green, greasy Limpopo River that the elephant's child visited. That Maine, today, is only a partial escape is no fault of the state, but of us, that so many of us go there. You may have your image of Maine, I will try and share mine. So let us begin, with the birth of that most unusual person, L. L. Bean, manufacturer and merchant, of Freeport, Maine, 04033.

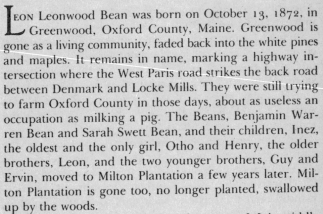

The Birth
of a Salesman

LEON Leonwood Bean was born on October 13, 1872, in Greenwood, Oxford County, Maine. Greenwood is gone as a living community, faded back into the white pines and maples. It remains in name, marking a highway intersection where the West Paris road strikes the back road between Denmark and Locke Mills. They were still trying to farm Oxford County in those days, about as useless an occupation as milking a pig. The Beans, Benjamin Warren Bean and Sarah Swett Bean, and their children, Inez, the oldest and the only girl, Otho and Henry, the older brothers, Leon, and the two younger brothers, Guy and Ervin, moved to Milton Plantation a few years later. Milton Plantation is gone too, no longer planted, swallowed up by the woods.

(It might as well be stated at the outset, L.L.'s middle name is Leonwood, not Linwood. *The Reader's Guide to Periodical Literature*, when indexing the memorable December 14, 1946, *Saturday Evening Post* feature on L. L. Bean, got it wrong in the listing. The article has it right, but the number of people who stopped with the index is considerable. There is, for example, a black Labrador retriever in Cincinnati, Ohio, named Linwood, on the owner's assumption that he had figured out the mystery of L. L. Bean. That is what happens when you ask your secretary [the dog in question belongs to the chief executive officer of Cincinnati Milacron, a major machine tool and robot manufacturer] to check something for you at the library. I will bet you a year's supply of dog food that there is no dog in North America named after either Mr. Sears or Mr. Roebuck, let alone by one of their middle names.)

L.L. is usually referred to as a down-easter, but as far as anyone knows, he never set a lobster trap or raked seaweed. He would eventually move to the coast, not very far down east at all, to run a dry goods store in Freeport. The childhood was in Oxford County, a place that has more to do with L.L. than mere genealogy.

Oxford County includes some of the hilliest, roughest country in Maine, outside the sudden rise of Mount Katahdin in Baxter State Park. It lies on the New Hampshire border, and includes a chunk of the White Mountain National Forest — of the Presidential Range, Mount Adams is in Maine. To the north, there are the high and lonely and not-much-hiked Caribou mountains.

So, it is not the big, sweeping, deep woods of the sportsmen's camps, nor the rockbound coast, neither is it the country of the pointed firs. It is hill country, a little bit claustrophobic, with mountains looming in the background, and there is one small mill town after another, making something, lumber or shoes or matches or toothpicks or paper, all based on waterpower, on the brooks tumbling down out of the White Mountains, and the massive rivers, the Androscoggin and the Swift, that arise across the border in New Hampshire.

It is good country for tinkerers, entrepreneurs, mill-wrights and mechanics. It is also — and this is difficult to explain by any geo-economic reason — perhaps the friendliest, most outgoing, part of Maine. There is an odd kind of outlooking, a curiosity about the world outside, about the places not so bound and confined by the high hills. This shows even in the locally famous and inexplicable names of some of the towns — Paris, Norway, Denmark, Mexico. Mexico is just across the Swift River from Rumford, one of the few towns in New England ever named for a Revolutionary War loyalist, Benjamin Thompson, Count Rumford.

Rumford was forgiven his politics for being a most practical inventor, interested in improving the heat and lighting of the common man's house, among other things — those are fit subjects in Maine, nine months of the year, and achievements worth honoring. It was perhaps prophetic that L. L. Bean was raised in a country-side that admired inventiveness; certainly, he was, all his life, a consummate tinkerer.

L.L., who would manage to go to school for eight or nine years without ever really learning how to spell, acquired a capacity to make money early in life, although, as became clear later, he was never worried about making a great deal of it. It was at the age of eleven, as he recalled almost seventy years later in his curious autobiography, *My Story,* that he was forced to make his first economic choice. He wanted to take the stage over to see the cattle show at Norway, Maine, and he wanted his father to give him the money to buy five steel traps. It was one or the other, his father told him; he could have the money but he would have to choose. L.L., who was called Lennie until he turned himself into a mail-order merchant, picked the traps, which accounted for themselves that first fall with five mink, five large and three baby muskrats. The mink sold for $1.25 each, he always remembered, the big muskrat for eight cents apiece, and the kits for five cents. He would continue, off and on for the next thirty years, to scratch a little extra money out of the woods.

The next year, 1884, both the parents died within days of each other, and the six Bean children were set out with friends of the family, or relatives, and scattered. Ervin, a younger brother, would be his off-and-on partner in the dry goods store in Freeport. Otho, the oldest brother, he remembered particularly because Otho had once been knocked down and spurred by a rooster, leaving a life-long scar in the middle of his forehead. Inez, the only sister, married into a local family that provided L.L. with hunting and fishing companions. Two other brothers, Henry and Guy, were occasional hunting partners. Guy, in later years, was the postmaster in Freeport, which made him the government-paid chief mail clerk for L. L. Bean.

L.L.'s life was typical of turn-of-the-century rural children — it was not so unusual, before antibiotics, for there to be orphaned children who would be passed along until they were old enough to work. Even then, L.L. would skip school, or duck out of work, to go hunting — killing his first deer at thirteen with a borrowed rifle. One forgets how short childhood could be back in the nineteenth century. At the age of fourteen, he took off into the woods, by logging train and foot, with a cousin a year older, camping in an abandoned lumber company building, just across the state line in New Hampshire. "My cousin shot his deer the second day," Bean recalled, "and went home. He promised to send someone up to stay with me. I was then only fourteen years old. The night he left me alone was the longest and most dismal of my life. I sat up all night in an old arm chair, in front of the old cook stove

with my clothes on, watching the fire through the grate."
(I had an uncle who, like all his brothers, was taken out
of school at that age and sent out of the small Montana
town the family lived in, to keep the ranch building. They,
at least, had a crank telephone that rang in the livery stable, if there was trouble. This one uncle, who was not, in
many ways, the most genial of the six brothers, was terribly lonely, too. But there was another ranch on the party
line, and every night, the ranch wife there would take her
telephone off the hook and play one or two pieces of music on an Edison cylinder phonograph so my uncle would
have some sound besides the wind to listen to.) After the
long night, L.L. managed to get his deer, a trophy buck,
and dragged it to the logging railroad. As would happen
then, and as it would happen to many Maine hunters for
the next eighty years, the engineer of the logging train
stopped for him, loaded the boy's deer in the cab of the
train, and stopped again at the old logging camp and tossed
it off for him. A few days later, L.L. always remembered
with satisfaction, two unsuccessful out-of-state hunters saw
the deer hanging outside the camp. These two sports offered the gangling lad twelve dollars for his deer if he
would haul it to their camp. L.L. pulled the deer five miles
on a sled over a snowy woods road and collected his money.
He was clearly over being homesick. He stopped in Has-
tings, Maine, bought some salt pork, bread, food, and a
pair of mittens, went back to his deer camp, and set a string
of traps, catching four marten (sables, he called them) and
a bobcat. He went home to his foster family in South Paris
with, as he put it, "the fur and most of my twelve dollars."
It was 1886, and it would be thirty years before he made
another nickel off the sport.

L.L. was migrating slowly toward the Maine coast as a
teenager, first a few miles southeast to an uncle's farm,

Sylvane Bean's place in West Minot. For two years he worked for twelve dollars a month hoeing beans and feeding cattle in the summer, and attending the local school in the winter — apparently always with time out for hunting and trapping. At eighteen, he found a better offer: sixteen dollars a month at a farm in East Hebron. At nineteen, he was entirely on his own, and out of Oxford County.

Kent's Hill, a small village a dozen miles north of the capital, Augusta, had a private academy with a commercial course. L.L. enrolled at the Kent's Hill Academy, and worked his way through a year's business course by selling soap. It was always his favorite story of his youth, and it was his last real success for twenty years, from 1891 until the idea of the Maine Hunting Shoe came to him in 1911.

What is surprising is that someone who was as good at selling soap as L.L. recalls himself being should not have struck it rich long before the age of forty. The mechanics of the soap scheme have been retold so often in Freeport that there are subtle variations — the version in *My Story* is, like all of L.L.'s expository prose, a mixture of terseness and vagueness.

Apparently what he did was very, very simple, and he managed to make the schoolboy into a minor-league wholesale salesman. He would begin on one Saturday by canvassing a neighborhood, leaving half-bars of hand soap, free, with the housewife. The following Saturday, he would retrace the route, taking orders for soap and then canvass a new neighborhood, again leaving the free sample. What he did next is more than a little confused by the passage of time and the retellings, but it was a clever scheme and it went approximately thusly: at the end of the school year, he took his accumulated orders to the local grocery stores, and pointed out to the storekeepers that he had sold this much soap to their customers. He would offer to turn the orders over to the store, for them to fill, if the store would give him a wholesale order for enough soap to fill his door-to-door presale and as much more. If, for example, a store's local customers had ordered two dozen boxes of soap in total, much of it in half-box orders, the store promised to buy four dozen boxes.

Now, he had orders for several hundred boxes of soap, collected from dozens of small stores in the Augusta area, and he was off to Portland on the train. There, he approached wholesale grocery jobbers with this fistful of orders, and offered to turn them over if the jobbers would order a whole boxcar load of soap. It was an ingenious scheme, built on direct sales, multiplied by store sales, and a guarantee, once he convinced the jobbers to order a carload, of acquiring the wholesale goods at the lowest possible price. He worked the soap market all summer, coordinating orders from Portland to Augusta, and then called it quits at the sales business.

That fall, 1892, he went to work in Bangor in a creamery, or as he would call it, a "butter factory." Nothing much happened in his life, he always said, between school and the invention of the Hunting Shoe. L.L.'s older brother, Otho, was a dry goods drummer, or factory representative, and he set up two younger brothers, L.L. and Ervin, in retail dry goods. Ervin ran a small store, backed with Otho's capital, in Freeport. For Lennie, Otho found a job clerking in a clothing store in Auburn, Maine.

A persistent rumor in New England, a story told by more than one old-timer, was that L.L. had served in the Spanish-American war, and, as the tale went, lent money to his fellow soldiers between paydays, at 10 percent interest. It is possible that a Bean was involved, but it was not L.L. Maine archives indicate that his two younger brothers, Ervin and Guy, enlisted in the Maine Militia's First Infantry Regiment, but there is no record that L.L. ever did military service.

Finally, as L.L. recalled, he moved back to Freeport in 1907 and, he wrote in *My Story*, "took over the store my brother, Ervin, had carried on while I was away. I managed to make a living until 1911." It is a little more complicated than that. In fact, as he told a reporter in 1960, he was going broke in Auburn, taking home twelve dollars a week, paying rent, with two young sons about to begin school, and a newborn daughter. L. L. Bean had taken a bride in 1898, a few years after he started clerking in Auburn. She was Bertha Porter, of Freeport, Maine. She was thirty-three; he was twenty-six. Three children were born during the years between the butter factory and the time he "returned to Freeport": Carl in 1900, Warren in 1902, and Barbara in 1907. The return to Freeport, his wife's hometown, was no triumph. They had to move in with the Porters, his wife's family. Ervin found something better to do, and Otho installed L.L. in the little dry goods and clothing store. He set L.L. up in business, as L.L. recalled, "to keep me from going on the town" — that is, from going on public charity. Things were not much better in Freeport. They could live rent-free with the Porters, but, L.L. remembered, "when I got $12 a week from that business, it was a plenty good week."

Barbara would marry John T. Gorman, of Passaic, New Jersey, in 1929, and become the mother of the current president of L. L. Bean, Leon Arthur Gorman, born in December 1934, and two other sons, John Thomas, Jr., born in 1930, and James Warren, born in 1932. Carl would not have children. Warren, who eventually more or less settled down, provided two granddaughters for L.L.,

16

Linda, born in 1941, and Diana, born in 1945. As L. L. Bean's is essentially an entirely family-held private corporation, this generation of grandchildren are shareholders in what is becoming the largest specialty mail-order house in the country — a business that if it were publicly held would have a paper worth of a third of a billion dollars.

Marriage, children, selling dry goods, nothing much happened to L. L. Bean until 1911. That, of course, is the year that he conceived of the leather-top, rubber-bottom Maine Hunting Shoe. But he was thirty-nine when he started to move from local merchant to merchandizer to the world, and the habits of the first four decades would never change. He would always be the absent manager, taking long vacations, disappearing for hunting and fishing trips in season, never much caring about profitability — that the system worked and the bills got paid would be enough for Leon Leonwood Bean.

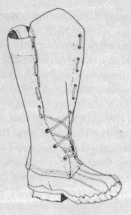

L.L. Has a Great Notion

L.L. Bean had bad feet, again, in the fall of 1911. Always reticent about his personal health, he never explained exactly what it was that hurt, itched, swelled up, or blistered. Certainly, he had one of the worst combinations of life-styles for the human foot — standing all day in the Freeport dry goods store (storeowners at the turn of the century did not sit down, lounge, or loll) and tramping the Maine woods.

The Maine deer-hunting season is particularly foul for the foot. It is a general principle of deer seasons that you delay it until the breeding season is well along, until the deer destined to survive have mated — the bucks spent, the does impregnated. This is November in Maine, a time when you can be sure that it will rain and snow, and the marshes will not yet be frozen, a time of wet feet and cold feet. Back in 1911, people tended to go hunting when they felt like it, game laws were vague, licenses were unheard of, and enforcement was nonexistent. Given a choice, any

sensible deer hunter would go in the first wet snow, be it
October or December.

The technology of 1911 knew of only one way to keep
dry, and that was rubber. Silicon-impregnated leather, and
the modern breathing, but waterproof, synthetics were sixty
and seventy years down the road. What L.L. wanted was
a dry foot, and he could get that easily by wearing rubber
galoshes, or a pair of the all-rubber boots that Maine
dairymen were already wearing in milking parlors. But you
can't walk in them. Well, you can walk, but you can't go
six miles up the ridges, trailing deer in a light snow cover.
Nobody ever made a rubber boot that fit around the ankle and the calf. Nobody, then or now, ever made a rubber boot that would snug down over a pair of socks and
keep your foot from sliding, and blistering, inside the shoe.
L.L. did try wearing a pair of pull-on rubber galoshes, with
three or four pairs of socks, and he managed to keep dry,
but he couldn't really handle the hills — there wasn't
enough bite, enough connection between the foot and the
shoe, for safe footing.

L.L., in the fall of 1911, was standing his store, miserable with his foot troubles. And what he was standing in
front of was a shelf full of pull-on, low-cut rubber galoshes. In his own words: "I took a pair of shoe rubbers
from the stock on the shelves and had a shoemaker cut
out a pair of 7 tops. The local cobbler stitched the whole
thing together."

The old country-boy, fix-it-with-baling-wire mentality
had made a great breakthrough, almost. He had the boots,
and they looked just fine to him. After he had the shoes
made, but before, as far as the record shows, he had ever
worn them on a hunting trip, he started boasting about
them. He "quite innocently praised" the new shoes to a
fellow who stopped in the store, an Edgar Conant, who

would be the first person ever to try them out. L.L. had a pair made for Edgar, who claimed to like them, and L.L. made his first sale, and, after cogitating on the problem, decided to go into the hunting shoe business.

What happened next was the beginning of the American direct-mail sporting goods business. This was already the great age of catalog mail-order sales — Sears & Roebuck and Montgomery-Ward were the largest merchants in the country (even today, Sears is the giant, a thousand times bigger than L. L. Bean). But there is a difference between mail-order and direct-mail sales, between the department-store-in-a-book (millions of American boys discovered female underwear for the first time in a Sears catalog), and directed marketing, where the seller finds the specific buyer, the prospect, through mailing lists. That, as much as the invention of the shoe, was the primary genius of L. L. Bean.

Having decided to manufacture and sell his Maine Hunting Shoe, which is what he called it from the beginning, L.L. went about the sales in a most practical manner. He would tell interviewers, in later years, that he wanted to reach hunters, so he went up to Augusta and copied down the names of Maine hunting license holders from the records at the Department of Fish and Game.

Then, as he recalled, he sold a hundred pairs of his Maine Hunting Shoes by mail, sometime over the summer of 1912. Unfortunately, the product was a total failure.

He took rubbers out of his store stock, and got two locals, Mr. and Mrs. Ted Goldrup, to cut out tops and stitch them to the rubbers. The soft, pliable rubber simply ripped apart after a few miles of hard going. As he recalled, he got back ninety out of the hundred boots, and was forced to refund the money. Thus, as he would tell the story, he had discovered the principle of directed mail, and also proven that the L. L. Bean guarantee was ironclad.

A summary of the story is the centerpiece of the L. L. Bean catalog, usually appearing on page 3.

Leon L. Bean founded our company in 1912, offering his new Maine Hunting Shoe to a list of Maine hunting license holders. He guaranteed his shoes "to give satisfaction in every way." The rubber bottoms separated from the leather tops on 90 of the first 100 pair. "L.L." kept his word and refunded the purchase price even tho' it nearly put him out of business. He then perfected his shoes and went on to establish our company based on quality outdoors products backed by an unconditional guarantee. In later years "L.L." wrote: "No doubt a chief reason for the success of this business is the fact that I tried on the trail practically every article I handle. If I tell you a knife is good for cleaning trout, it is because I found it so. If I tell you a wading boot is worth having, very likely you might have seen me testing it out at Merrymeeting Bay."

There is a small problem, however, with this whole story. The mailing list could not have existed. Bean certainly could have used a license holders list, but not until after the 1917 fall hunting season, when Maine instituted its first licenses. However he had sold his first Maine Hunting Shoes, and whether the hundred-sold, ninety-returned story is entirely accurate, Bean did realize he had something that would sell if he could get the product perfected. The first boots, made of rubber galoshes, were entirely unsatisfactory, and so was the basic material. Not only was the galosh rubber too soft to stitch to the leather uppers, but the pull-on rubbers had, as you can imagine, a concavity in them to accept the heel of a dress shoe. Bean just cut up pieces of felt to fill in that hole.

He decided to have a rubber bottom made expressly for his purpose, and borrowed four hundred dollars from his brother Otho to place an order with the U.S. Rubber

Company of Boston. Otho, who had set L.L. up in business, remained the best hope for borrowing money. But U.S. Rubber was unwilling to make up a series of lasts — molds for the rubber bottoms — at their own expense, and they would cost considerably more than four hundred dollars. L.L. returned to Freeport, borrowed some more money, and went back to Boston in 1913 with the cash, and a promise that if U.S. Rubber would cooperate, they would both make money. They did, with Bean's being U.S. Rubber's single largest "rubbers" customer until the mid-1960s, when production stopped in Boston (and most of the United States) and Bean switched the rubber-bottoms account to the La Crosse Rubber Company of La Crosse, Wisconsin.

However he was selling, and most of it was by mail, Bean was able to see his future lay in the mail-order, not the retail dry goods business. In January 1918, he sold the dry goods store to spend his entire energy on mail order. Later that year, he took out United States and Canadian patents on the touted "reinforced back stay" that allegedly keeps the Maine Hunting Shoe from irritating the wearer's Achilles tendon.

To return to the confusion over the mailing list of Maine license holders, the putative beginning of the business and the source of the first hundred customers, I suspect it is just a confusion in L.L.'s mind between the year he started in the mail-order business part-time, 1912, and 1918, the year he got into it full-time. There is no reason to believe that he fabricated the whole story of using licenses as the source of prospective customers. For although it is not accurate in fact, it is perfectly true in explaining the growth of his fledgling company. What is important to understanding the whole phenomenon of L. L. Bean, Inc., is to realize that it has never been a *Maine* business, it has always been a company dependent on the sports, the out-of-staters. This fits perfectly with the famous, if spurious, hunting license list.

In 1917, Maine issued its first hunting licenses — to *nonresidents only* — for the princely sum of two dollars. They sold 7,500 of them. It was indeed, the perfect mailing list for L.L. Mainers, by and large, go hunting and fishing in the clothes they wear to work, or, if they are sedentary office workers, in the clothes they wear to take the garbage to the dump and to run the snow blower. The person who needs something special to wear in the woods is, by definition, the sport. He needs the waterproof shoe, and he needs the chamois cloth shirt so thick that the mosquitos have trouble biting through it. He needs the perfect knife for cleaning trout because he's not home, where the kitchen drawer has a perfectly good knife in it. He needs the jelly-spreader to make sandwiches; he, and he alone, really *needs* L. L. Bean. The proprietor of a dry goods store in a small village was the perfect mediator between the woods and the sports — he was of the woods, but not in them, his forays were not unlike theirs, except, perhaps, he had more woods sense and didn't have to take the train to get to Maine.

The out-of-state license list was the kick that the business needed. In 1918 he could hire a full-time bookkeeper and cashier, Miss Hazel Goldrup, daughter of the team that was stitching his newly designed rubbers to the leather tops. By 1919 he had moved across the street from the original dry goods store to the present location of the Bean retail store, and he had leased the top floor of the business building for a warehouse. In 1920 he bought the building. All of this had been accomplished on the strength of direct-mail sales, especially through the out-of-state license list.

The pattern had been set: it would be out-of-staters. Bean began his practice of pouring all the profit back into advertising, placing ads in all the national hunting and fishing magazines.

With one brief exception, L. L. Bean's life, from the day he bought the building until he died, would be inseparable from the company's life. He had been known, all his life, as "Lennie," but by the mid-1920s, he wanted people to call him "L.L." Lennie was the store clerk, L.L. was the manufacturing executive from Freeport. The only time, for the next forty years, that he turned his attention away from hunting, fishing, and running the catalog store, were the war years, when he served briefly as a consultant to the U.S. Army and Navy, and when a significant part of his manufacturing capacity was devoted to war work — he was in no sense a war-profiteer, nor was he a bulwark of the arsenal of defense — he did fill orders for several hundred thousand military versions of the insulated Maine Hunting Shoe, and manufactured a few thousand similar boots with deck soles for aircraft carrier flightline crews.

He was proud of his brief service as a clothing consultant to the War Department — and included, in the first editions of *My Story*, a photocopy of his personnel action form, which noted that he would be paid $25 per diem as an "Expert" in the research and development branch of the military planning division of the department. As later editions appeared, he included his letter of commendation, dated 19 December 1945, from Georges F. Doriot, a brigadier general and director of the military planing division. For if L.L. had not manufactured much materiel for the services, he had offered his advice, especially, as the letter noted, "in connection with such important items for the soldier as winter footgear, more specifically Shoe Pacs. . . . No one realizes more than this office the importance of the time, effort, and skill which have been so fully devoted by your company in helping this office to improve this item for use by troops in the field."

L.L. himself, quite typically, was less interested in the Shoe Pac (an item that never gained the affections of the GIs who suffered through the winter war in Europe in them) than in two other contributions. They were classic Bean contributions — the first was both parsimonious and practical; the second was typical, make-do, country ingeniousness.

The problem with the leather-top, rubber-bottom Shoe Pacs was simple. The army had always liked extremely high-topped boots, a carryover from cavalry days (cavalry trained and experienced officers, like George Patton, were the army equivalent of the navy's "destroyer-trained" officers; those were the natural first steps to elite commands), and from the riding tradition at West Point. The ordinary combat boot of the prewar army was sixteen inches tall (and authentically recreated in that best of movies about the prewar army, *From Here to Eternity*, with Frank Sinatra, Montgomery Clift, and Burt Lancaster in their hightoppers). Bean went to Washington in September of 1942, to serve on a special committee looking at recommended designs for cold-weather Shoe Pacs. "There was quite a difference of opinion on footwear," Bean recalled, "especially on the height of the leather top rubber-bottomed boots which were being considered. Practically all the other members of the committee were quite a bit younger than I was [he was sixty-one] and came from the West and South. They were strongly in favor of a 16″ or 18″ boot, whereas I, coming from a colder climate and having tramped through the woods for many years, knew from experience that a high boot would bind the leg muscles of a man who had to be on his feet all day, so that he would soon be lame and sore and unable to walk at all."

Bean argued long and hard for the ten-inch height (his

personal favorite, and the best-selling model of the Maine Hunting Shoe before the low-cut, street-wear models took over in the 1970s), but, he acknowledged, "we finally compromised and a 12″ boot was adopted," and "the result was that later we were given a large order for 12″ leather top rubbers. These were made on the pattern of our Maine Hunting Shoe." A similar Shoe Pac was used on wet and icy decks, he wrote, "and it was necessary at times for a man to get out of them in a hurry before he went into the water." The committee was asked to come up with a "quick release" contraption, and it was L.L.'s son Carl who solved the problem, very simply, according to Bean. "Instead of lacing the five eyelets from the bottom up, a small loop was made in the laces, and they were laced from the top eyelet down. In an emergency a man grasped the small loop at the top and the laces came out, leaving him free to kick off the boots."

(I have pondered that explanation at length. I have made inquiries of formal naval persons who are unaware of the technique. However, there is at least one way to do it: Run the lace through both top eyelets. Form a loop with one side of the lace long enough to run from the top eyelet down to the bottom eyelet on one side, and enough longer to leave a small loop above the top eyelet. Then lace the boots from top to bottom, and, on the side where the loop lies next to the eyelets, run the lace around the loop and back through the eyelet, instead of passing it directly around the boot material through the eyelet. Then, if you pull on the top of the loop that is sticking up above the top eyelet, you will pull out the only support that the laces have on that side, and the boot will be free.)

Other products for the military came from the Bean experience, including a light, but still practical, axe, the one manufactured by Snow and Neally of Bangor, Maine, and still carried in some editions of the catalog as "our best axe." His other major order was for a version of the Bean's Brief Case, the simple leather and zipper handleless item that has appeared in the catalog for the past fifty years. The wartime model was much larger overall, with internal dividers, intended for officers in navigation schools, "to hold their charts, instructions, etc. We finally came to a decision on the proper size, etc., and were given an order to make up 40,000 of them. Later we heard from many of the officers who used them, and how they carried the cases all around the world after their training was completed."

Bean's business was virtually unaffected by the war — the military orders, small by the standards of major manufacturers, picked up the slack in civilian orders. The shoe rationing (mail-order customers were required to send in the appropriate ration stamps with their orders) that hurt the civilian business was neatly matched by the ration-free priority of the military business. Although busy, Bean did not add a single foot of manufacturing or storage space to his holdings from 1941 to 1947. It is apparently the case that he spent as much time fishing in Florida each winter as he did working for the government. He was in no hurry to expand the business as the war wound down in his sixty-fourth year.

L. L. Bean Finds Himself

L. L. Bean, like any famous human being, would eventually have trouble separating his public image from reality. The one thing that remained fixed throughout his later life was his self-image as a trader — a merchant.

His father was the same, a part-time farmer who spent most of his energy on livestock trading and minor-league swaps with the neighbors. The old man would lay in barrels of sugar in the fall, and trade with the neighbors in the long winters of Oxford County. L.L., later, would romanticize that when he told an interviewer that "There were five of us boys, and I guess we were all the same way [as the father]. Didn't any of us ever put on overalls." Of course, they did, and L.L. spent at least five years hoeing beans and mowing hay and feeding cattle before he could break away from the farm life, first as a door-to-door salesman, later as the sometimes partner, sometimes sole owner, of the torpid little dry goods store in Freeport.

The original self-image, the one that was fully created before he had the idea of going into mail-order selling, was that he, after all, was a genuine expert on hunting and fishing. The famous line in the old catalog about trout flies is typical: "We have made a survey of hundreds of brook-trout flies to determine how many we could eliminate. We have decided that nine flies in two sizes are all that are necessary and in many cases four or five will answer nicely."

That is the public image of thrift, wisdom, and local knowledge that meant Maine to visiting sports. But L.L. could not quit there. Sensitive to the public image, he would have to feed it, and maintain it, long after the public had fully formed its perception.

L.L., for one thing, had no perceptible sense of humor beyond that country slyness that would make him sit at the top of the stairs in the retail store and count off the customers on a clicker. He was much amused that they did not know who the old man in the chair really was.

Other people could make him laugh. He was fond of collecting the odder sorts of letters, and waving them at the interviewers who started to pay attention to him after World War II. A few were reprinted in *My Story*, and they give a reasonable insight into L.L.'s sense of the comic:

> *Dear Sir:*
> *Enclosed find check for which please send me one Bean's Pack Basket and one Pack Basket cover. Outside of my wife, this is the handiest piece of equipment a man could take to the woods.*

Another, a postcard from a rural route box holder on Wisconsin's upper peninsula, was reproduced photographically for full effect:

> *Dear Sir:*
> *Send for shoes; 4 weeks pass no shoes: Write letter, 6 weeks pass, no shoes. Write another letter, next day shoes come. Shoes O:K. Me O:K. Hope you O:K.*

He was garrulous, affable, and could, like most Maine natives, shift in and out of dialect pronunciation. He was not, however, a storyteller. He had none of the down-east type of humor — the long, meandering, shaggy-dog humor of coastal fishermen. His professions, store clerk and salesman, precluded him from exercising the laconic, bitter humor of the backwoods and rural neighborhoods. There is nothing of L.L. himself that is deliberately humorous in either *My Story* or *Hunting-Fishing and Camping*.

It must have been apparent to the old man, as he struggled to the close of his brief manuscript for *My Story*, that he was not holding up his end of the bargain, to be a true Maine person, and so he did the obvious, and the necessary. He retold what is certainly the oldest, most widely circulated, of all Maine stories (which means all rural English stories; a version appears in two Arthurian romances):

> A few years ago, while fishing in Northern Maine, I got mixed up in my direction while attempting a short-cut to camp. I finally ran into a barefoot boy [it, of course, has to be a barefoot one] and started asking him questions without admitting the fact that I did not know the way home. Unable to get an intelligent reply that would help me out of my predicament, I finally said, "I guess you don't know much anyway, do you?"
>
> The boy answered, "No, but I'm not lost."

But L.L.'s personal style in humor was of the purely sly. He got most of his fun out of operating in disguise — wandering around the store and listening to people talk about him, or sitting at the top of the stairs counting the customers, anonymously. His favorite story for interviewers in the 1940s came out of his brief work in Washington, D.C., as an adviser to the quartermaster corps on outdoor clothing. It was the opening anecdote in the first really useful national recognition Bean's got — the December 14, 1946, issue of *The Saturday Evening Post.*

During the war, a general leaving the Pentagon Building found himself sharing a taxicab to downtown Washington with a civilian. In the casual taxicab conversation that developed, the civilian named his home town as Freeport, Maine. The general's interest brightened at once.

"Freeport?" he said. "That's L. L. Bean's town."

"Ay-yah," the man from Maine agreed. "'Tis."

"There's a man I'd sure like to meet," said the general. "L. L. Bean. I discovered him four or five years ago, and I've been buying from him ever since. By George, it's wonderful the way that man figures out just what you need for hunting and fishing. You hunt or fish?"

"Ay-yah," said the Freeporter, "do a lot of it. Always use Bean's things too. Now, you take Bean's duck-hunting coat —"

The conversation had hit high gear, and continued, an exchange of hunting and fishing experiences, well interlarded with tributes to the equipment and clothing sold by the mail-order house of L. L. Bean, all the way to the hotel where the civilian was getting out. As he stepped from the cab, he extended his hand. "Pleased to meet you, general," he said. "My name's L. L. Bean."

Instructive as the story may be about Bean's idea of a real thigh-slapper, it is more to the point that when Bean's was a tiny business, grossing less than a million dollars, it had already established itself as a personality — you did not buy boots from L. L. Bean, Inc., of Freeport, Maine — you bought boots from a Mr. L. L. Bean, who lived in Freeport. As the *Post* reporter grasped, perhaps more than Bean himself, Bean's customers regarded him, and the company, as a form of special revelation.

> . . . it seems to be an almost universal illusion among his customers, as it was with the general, that Bean is a personal discovery, to be cherished as a rare and rich curiosity. Bean, as a shrewd businessman, does his best to foster this impression. . . .

Seldom has a personality so dominated a catalog. The only even remotely comparable mail-order master of Bean's era was the irrepressible Carl Herter, a younger man who ran a successful fishing-tackle business by mail, a company now long defunct that began to founder when Herter became obsessed with the communist menace and the inevitability of a third world war. The introduction to the Herter's catalog became a diatribe combined with survivalist advice — Bean might sell you waterproof matches so that you boil tea in the woods; Herter, toward the end, was selling you matches so that you could survive until the nuclear counterstrikes had destroyed Moscow.

Bean, of course, was middle-aged (thirty-nine was perhaps older than middle age in those years before antibiotics and palliative drugs) before he founded the business, and past retirement age before anyone in the news media realized he was a story — he was, in any case, long past the age when he could mold his character, or his behavior, to be marketable. He could be shrewd, he could crank out his perverse, if direct, catalog language, but he could not change his basic personality. From 1946 to his death in 1967, L.L. didn't change, and the business didn't grow an inch — the gross sales moved from $1 million to $3 million, but twenty years of post–World War II inflation should have increased the gross to $6 million, had he kept pace with the times.

The least appropriate description of his character is the most common one — that he was a down-east storekeeper. The illusion that he was simply running a catalog version of a Maine country store is purely, absolutely, in the minds of the beholders. A country store might, as Bean's did and does, sell a standard line of knives, in this case the ubiquitous Chicago Cutlery Company line of knives, but only L. L. Bean would have the nerve to take the small boning knife, sew up a leather blade cover for it, and call it a Knife for Cleaning Trout. It is that self-centered audacity that separated Bean from his contemporaries, that absolutely incredible ego, that sense that he could do no wrong, have no bad ideas, that made him the personal discovery for his customers.

If Bean's Trout Knife was a Chicago standard in a new dress, the entire catalog was a monument to his self-assurance. Back in the 1940s, when the catalog had only ninety-six pages spring and fall, the name Bean appeared in it 360 times, and the editorial "We," as in "We do not know of a warmer, more nearly waterproof fabric," another 125. It was an astonishing performance for that more reticent age, when the few corporate spokesmen in the world were creations of advertising departments, like General Mills' "Betty Crocker." If a hundred marketing managers have tried to imitate the personal style of L. L. Bean, it has been approximated only rarely, and probably best by Frank Perdue, who burst onto the nation's consciousness in 1980 as the tough man who knew how to grow a tender chicken.

Bean succeeded in doing the impossible with his catalog — he turned the message into the medium. Ninety-six pages of black and white pictures and captions, tucked inside a badly drawn color cover, were perceived as a human personality — the inarticulate, badly educated, nearly illiterate L. L. Bean had managed to get *a* personality, not necessarily his own, into print. Whoever it was inside those pages, it did not much appeal to the people of Maine. They, after all, had real country stores to go to, and did not need to pay the premium for L.L.'s advice, purchasing, and advertising and mailing costs.

There are Maine country stores that do resemble an L. L. Bean catalog laid out on shelves, but it is hard to tell if they stock some of the goods because they ought to, or because people expect to see them in a Maine store. But there is a remarkable difference in the contents of a real store and a Bean catalog — once you get past the boxes of (Canadian-made) rubber-bottomed, leather-topped footwear, the stacks of crushable felt hats, and the piles of (Woolrich) chamois cloth shirts. You get to stacks of real axes, not the little lightweights that Bean sells, you get to quarts of outboard and chainsaw motor oil. And most of all, you get past the hype, the pitch, the oversell that characterizes Bean. The real Maine storekeeper is reticent, and promises nothing.

Up in Greenville, on the shores of Moosehead Lake, there is a real Maine institution, Sanders Store (which now, rather coyly, reminds you that it is an "old country store") that deals with both summer folk and real people. I once overheard one of the locals asking if they had a particular item in stock and, hearing that they didn't, ask if they would order him one. "Nope," was the answer.

"Why not?"

"Won't get one for months. When it does come in, the quality will be down, the price will be up, and you won't want it anyhow."

In small-town clothing stores, there have always been two kinds. There were stores that sold Stetson hats and Pendleton wool shirts, and there were stores that didn't. There never was a store like Bean's, that sold its own stuff exclusively, and made you believe it was as good as you could get.

Through the 1930s, '40s and '50s, there was only one product in the Bean's catalog that wasn't Bean's best, and that was the ubiquitous Hudson Bay Blanket, of which Bean sold the cheapest version. No one else, for years, could penetrate the aura. He used to give credit to "a Tribe of State-of-Maine Indians" for weaving Bean's Pack Basket, or acknowledge that Bean's Maine Woods Compass was manufactured "by the most reliable company we know of," but that was the limit. It would be late in his life, and early in the employment of his grandson, Leon Gorman, now the president of Bean's, before the company would credit Bangor's Snow and Neally as manufacturer of "Our Best Axe" (which, by the way, was not Snow and Neally's best axe, and since it was the only axe in the catalog, might reasonably be admitted to being Bean's best).

No, the old man was unique. He managed to create the image of himself, and put the image in print. He was the man from Maine who knew it all and, unlike most of them, would tell you. Perhaps that was the secret, and the reason it doesn't work when it is imitated, that a Mainer, of all people, was willing to tell you the secret. A New Yorker who knew it all would be no surprise, there would be no feeling that you had penetrated to the very soul of a New Yorker who had such a deal for you.

Bean, after all, was the man you were looking for — what could have come across in print as outrageous know-it-all egotism was saved by the inelegant, practically suffering, artless prose. He seemed, as was commonly said of a wise man, to be a fellow who knew a thing or two. You would not get a bum steer. You would not go wrong.

A Few Notes on the Organization of the L. L. Bean Catalog

THE curious structure of the L. L. Bean catalog always bemuses journalists — and they always manufacture a justification for the helter-skelterness of it. This was frequently done with L.L.'s help, as he was fond of explaining the obvious. The new catalog, for better or worse, has some logic to it. The Maine Hunting Shoe display is always the centerfold, and men's and women's clothing is reasonably well grouped — no longer does one find men's shirts in six different places. But the new catalog is an imitation of reality, it is the catalogs of the 1930s, '40s, and '50s that reveal so much about the mind of L. L. Bean, if they are taken at face value.

Various writers, "discovering" Bean's in the 1940s and 1950s, concluded that the organization of the catalog was a deliberate attempt to force the customer to browse through every item along the way to the merchandise he actually wanted to purchase. L.L. encouraged them in this delusion. "There is Yankee method, however, to the apparent madness," *Newsweek* announced in 1961. "Bean omits the index from his catalog because he figures each page is worth $10,000 in sales and he doesn't want to waste the space. Customers searching for one item in the catalog, moreover, are lured by others en route; one Texan [an oft-repeated story that has never been verified] simply ordered 'everything on pages 8 through 64.' "

One would be stuck with that explanation. if Bean had not decided to write two books — *My Story* and *Hunting-Fishing and Camping*, both printed by the company that used to produce his catalogs, the Dingley Press of Freeport.

My Story begins reasonably enough with his birth — though not without a plug for the company. "Greenwood . . . was the first place the name 'L. L. Bean' ever appeared — the town clerk put it on my birth certificate on October 13, 1872." Four brief paragraphs later, he is an orphan, and before the first page is done, Bean has begun to describe his first hunting trip — it is the major anecdote in his summary of his life before the founding of the company — "My life up to the age of forty years was most uneventful, with a few exceptions."

In two reasonably chronological pages, Bean makes his way to the age of nineteen and a fling at door-to-door sales, which he gave up in return for the job at a Bangor butter factory in the fall of 1892. At that point, any reasonable resemblance to a chronology begins to disappear, and the *Story* becomes as tangled a web as a vintage catalog.

At the end of one paragraph it is 1892 and he's in Bangor, and the next paragraph begins:

"In 1907 I moved back to Freeport and took over the store my brother, Ervin, had carried on while I was away." Away where? you may ask.

After recounting the invention of the Maine Hunting Shoe, Bean moves rapidly on from 1911 in the following sequence:

In June, 1917, I moved across the street to my present quarters. . . .

. . . meantime I hired Hazel Goldrup, the daughter of my cutter and stitcher. . . . [She] deserves more credit for the success of my mail order business . . . than any other one person. She was the bookkeeper, cashier, auditor and boss of the office. When I went on my hunting trips, I never worried about the business.

Bertha Porter Bean, mother of my three children, Carlton, Warren and Barbara, died in May, 1939, at the age of 73.

The section headed with the dates: "1920–1932," opens with the statement that "The basement of the store, 40′ × 25′, was my first factory. . . . This was in 1914, and the business was entirely local."

A few pages later, he has moved on to another era, as the crosshead on the page indicates ("1934–1947"), and the focus there is on the incorporation of the company with the first "officers elected Nov. 16, 1934 . . . L. L. Bean, President and Treasurer; Carl Bean [his son, but not so noted] Vice President and Assistant Treasurer; Jack Gorman, my son-in-law, Vice President and Clothing Buyer; and Warren Bean, my son, Clerk." And continues on without a break, or a pause, or any apology, back to the 1890s: "My home, Milton Plantation, had one hotel and one general store. The hotel was owned by R. T. Allen and the store by M. T. Look, better known as Rat Tail Allen and Mouse Tail Look."

The next eighty pages of the book are stitched together with family photographs, pictures of L.L. and dead moose, L.L. and dead bear, L.L. and dead deer. The autobiography continues with another series of outdoors anecdotes — getting lost in the woods, duck hunting, and pointing out that the second Mrs. Bean, Claire, once caught "an 8-foot sailfish in less than an hour after having her line over. This was a feat which many sportsmen had hoped and tried for a long time to accomplish, without success."

And then, with the same logic as the catalog, Bean continues the story of his life with the official report of the Freeport School Committee of 1918 on the new high school building, constructed for a cost of $28,600. The committee, of which he was acting chairman, brought the building in at cost, with an unexpended balance of $7.49.

The biography ends where an L. L. Bean story should end — the last recorded words of the old merchant on his life were:

> In March of 1947 we received an order from a customer in St. Marys, Pennsylvania, with a check for $426.40 enclosed. The order called for 51 items from page 7 to page 64, the last page in the catalog that year.

My Story was written when Bean was sixty-seven, the earlier *Hunting-Fishing and Camping* in 1942, when he was merely sixty. The earlier book is slightly more organized, but not overwhelmingly so, and laced with many of the pictures that illustrate *My Story*, particularly the photographs of Bean and his quarry. In its own way, it gives as clear a picture of the man as the autobiography.

Written in pure Bean style, a creative mixture of ungrammatical but somehow accurate English, it begins with a chapter on deer hunting, and with these questions.

> The first thing to decide: Where shall I go? Second: How many do I want to make up the party?
> Where to go is the most important question to settle. You will find your answer in Chapter 37.

The answer is to try and arrive at a place the week that the first snow is expected: "Of course you may miss the snow but at that time of year the leaves are well off and you are almost sure to get rain or snow that you can get around quietly."

Hunting-Fishing and Camping is not really a book about how to do these things on your own. It focuses on the hunting party, and it frequently assumes the presence of a guide and a hunting camp. It amounts to an attempt to break away from the backwoods. The boy who worked his way off the farm to the commercial academy wanted to be a sportsman, not a woodsman — a gentleman who went hunting, not a hunter who ran a sporting goods store. In that, he was like his customers — he was a Sport at heart. Many of the pictures in *Hunting-Fishing* of L.L. and his family, and L.L. and his friends, not only have the mandatory arrangements of dead ducks and drying fish, but they also have guides — never identified, just, well, guides.

It seems incongruous that L. L. Bean's catalog would include a whole line of men's dress shirts, and it seems impossible that they could claim "These are the shirts worn by L. L. Bean on his way to and from his hunting camps," but it is not. Gentlemen — and L.L. wanted to be one, made himself one, became the squire of Freeport, not just local merchant, but public citizen, chairman of town committees, and promoter of local industry, real estate broker — no, gentlemen do not drive to camp looking like an advertisement for the National Rifle Association.

"I am taking the liberty of recommending just what I wear," L.L. wrote in *Hunting-Fishing;* and he did, including:

Underwear: Two union suits same as worn at home.
Pants: One pair medium weight all wool with knit or zip-

per bottoms. Also wear from home your heaviest business suit.

If Bean's ever wants to sell three-piece suits (joining, say, the Orvis Fishing Tackle company into a complete department store for Preppies), they have the founder's blessing — everything you needed, for a proper sporting expedition, would include a blue serge suit.

Bean's inveterate thriftiness (the man who paid the minimum wage was the same man who brushed elbows with the rich and famous in his store) comes through, and his earthiness.

"For deer hunting I believe it is very important to wear partly red coat and cap but if you don't care to go to the expense, pin a red handkerchief over cap and on back of coat to avoid accidental shooting," he cautioned his readers. Maine suffered for years from a plethora of deer-hunting accidents, finally becoming the first northern New England state to require the wearing of blaze orange gear during the season, a move that recalcitrant New Hampshire and Vermont still refuse to follow.

"*Handkerchiefs:*," Bean wrote: "Six red bandanas. Do not use white in woods. I also recommend colored toilet paper." He was not jesting. More than one hunter has been shot, usually fatally, while attending to that need with a flash of white tissue that brings a shot from a nearby hunter.

"Some old hunters," Bean remarked sourly, "do not wear red because they believe that it frightens deer. This is a mistaken idea."

Hunting-Fishing could have been turned into a plug for everything Bean sold, and certainly his sales of red and blue bandannas could not have been hurt by his advice. Many a man who would not, could not, shoot a deer or

be in the woods in deer season, would find himself ordering a real Maine handkerchief. But *Hunting-Fishing* re-
stricts itself to a few pictures of camping gear spread out,
or clothing laid out on a blanket, all of it available from
L. L. Bean, but none of it so advertised, so identified. The
one particular chance he had to list his own gear was
stymied by the war effort — when *Hunting-Fishing* was
published in 1942, the war effort had already banned the
sale of "hunting" clothing, and Bean had to change the
copyrighted Maine Hunting Shoe into a nonhunting item
for the duration. In listing his personal clothing, he was
obliged to tell the reader to bring "One pair 12" Leather
Top Rubbers," the wartime euphemism for the Maine
Hunting Shoe.

The book does not speak to our time at all, although
some of the advice is reasonably useful — the brief section on how to cast the artificial fly is not really a subject
much improved on by fancier authors, although you would
not want to tell *them* that. The number of fishermen who
can actually cast a fly from one horseshoe stake to the other
(forty feet) are still less than half the anglers, in spite of
all the improvements in equipment and instruction.

But what it does remind us of is the era when the man
with a De Soto sedan and time on his hands could load
up with canned goods and flour and a bottle of syrup and
head for camp, or, if he was a real Sport, just pack his
clothes and head for the sporting camp, where those
anonymous guides and their wives would take care of the
meals. It was a simple age, and thirty-nine chapters in
eighty pages probably did tell you all you needed to know
about Maine's outdoor life.

But the helter-skelter prose, the organization by intuition, the dogged insistence on the value of experience over
theory, characterize the mind of the real L. L. Bean, and
the catalog he created.

The First Decade: L.L. Searches for a Market

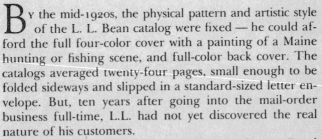

By the mid-1920s, the physical pattern and artistic style of the L. L. Bean catalog were fixed — he could afford the full four-color cover with a painting of a Maine hunting or fishing scene, and full-color back cover. The catalogs averaged twenty-four pages, small enough to be folded sideways and slipped in a standard-sized letter envelope. But, ten years after going into the mail-order business full-time, L.L. had not yet discovered the real nature of his customers.

The company was titled "L. L. Bean, Manufacturer," and the product line made it clear that L.L. had not yet recognized that his real market was not the woodsmen of Maine, but the Sports of Boston and New York. He was still offering work shoes and boots, and logger's calks that could be screwed into the bottom of the work boots — a kind of do-it-yourself logger's footwear factory. Calks would disappear from the catalog in a few years, because the whole point of Bean's footwear is that you can wear it anywhere — out to start the car, into the office on a snowy winter's day. But while Bean was still sorting out his products to match his market, he had firmly developed his maddened prose style.

Technical descriptions brought out the best in misplaced modifiers and missing antecedents. He was working through the old U.S. Rubber Company of Boston, and selling their better line of hip waders, which he preferred to call the Maine Duck Hunting Boot. The boot included a rubber strap mounted on the inside — designed to hold the boot by constriction above the calf muscle — and a loose strap that could be used to keep the fit tight by wrapping it around the outside of the boot at the ankle: Bean included a diagram of the boot "*Showing how leg is held in place when worn below the knee.*" The advertising copy boasted that "These straps are a big improvement not found on any other boot."

As with many items, Bean promoted the idea of testing out the hip-boot material before making the purchase — "Send for free sample of rubber and try to puncture it with stick or pencil."

Huckstering was a little bolder in the early days. The Cold Proof Duck Hunting Coat was not just warm, it was "about 100 per cent perfect. The protection it gives to the neck and ears on cold days is worth the price of the coat." Not only did Bean's usual guarantee apply to the $12.50 Duck Hunting Coat, but L.L. added that he "would like to have you see this garment. Order one and if you do not keep it we will pay charges both ways and return your money."

Bean's most important image, that of New England thriftiness, was a theme he would play to the best of his ability. The Maine Camp Slipper (long since gone from the catalog) was a matter of medical necessity at the right price. "To keep feet in best condition," L.L. warned, "Hunting Shoes or Boots should be removed on reaching

44

camp. The Maine Camp Slipper weighs only 6 oz. per pair and are . . . made roomy over instep for woolen stockings." But this real bargain ($1.75, free delivery), he explained, was made possible by his thrift: "Price is low, as uppers are made of pieces too small for hunting shoe tops." Snowshoe rigging, the leather contraption that is supposed to hold the boot to the snowshoe, was also made of "waste pieces that are too small for our Hunting Shoes, we are able to make a light weight high-grade rigging at the low price of $1.25." A Boy's Winter Sport Cap (a simpler verson of what are now usually called trooper's caps) was "gotten out to use up pieces of leather and lamb skin that are too small for our Men's Cap. We originally planned to sell to dealers only but it has proved so popular we have decided to offer it direct to consumer."

Clothing styles ran heavily to modified knickers, or variations on World War I military clothing — the Maine Duck Hunting Pant, the Plain Gray Hunting Pant, the bottoms of the Two Piece Hunting Suit, and the New Plaid Hunting Pant all were cut short, with lacings at the bottom "so as to fit smoothly under stockings or leggings. . . . For tucking into shoes they are a big improvement over the ordinary hem bottom pants."

The description of the Maine Duck Hunting Coat took considerable reading before one realized it was not a coat for hunting ducks, it was a coat made out of "highest grade olive green duck . . . the toughest fabric known." In brown duck, it would evolve into today's Maine Hunting Coat, a garment intended for upland game hunters.

The centerpiece of the catalog was fixed, one of the few things that has not changed in sixty years — a full page of the Maine Hunting Shoe, refined virtually to what it is today, with the "patent backstay . . . a positive protection against heel cord chafing." Bean realized that heel cord

(Achilles tendon) chafing was a problem with poorly fitted boots, and remarked: "To the experienced hunter I need not say any more." But, since he was beginning to reach an audience outside that fraternity, he cautioned the tyros: "To those who are making their first trip to the big woods, be sure and get a shoe that will not chafe the heel cords."

In addition to the Hunting Shoe, a half-dozen items from the 1920s have survived. Bean's Maine Snow-shoe is better spelled these days, but it is still described in the original prose: "If there is a better Snow-shoe made we certainly would like to see it"; however, the "best cowhide" filling is no longer "cured by a secret process that positively prevents sagging."

The Ladies' Indian House Slipper has gone the way of all flesh, and taken its "furette" trimming and hand beading with it. In the '20s, Bean had not quite formed his utter distaste for gewgaws, and remarked that "after experimenting with a lot of fancy house slippers, . . . settled on this one as the neatest and most practical. It is a State of Maine souvenir that would be highly prized as a gift by anyone."

That staple of the current Bean's catalog, and every one else's, the Hudson Bay Blanket, moved L.L. to near inarticulateness in the '20s — "so high grade and handsome that we cannot do them justice on paper." He did note that "These blankets were formerly marketed under the name of Hudson Bay, which name is discontinued [by Bean] on account of objections being made by the Hudson Bay Company of Canada."

By 1923, Bean had realized that among other problems with the Maine Hunting Shoe, it was practically impossible to wear without an innersole. Bean's still sells innersoles, but hardly pushes them — a brief note near the current listing of Hunting Shoes suggests them, but doesn't demand that you buy a pair. That, of course, is because by far the largest number of Hunting Shoe purchasers use them to walk to the bus in, or go to the dump in, not to walk a dozen miles on frozen ground. Bean devoted an entire page to the subject of innersoles in the 1920s:

> After experimenting for years we find that it is just as necessary to have a stiffening in the shank of a rubber or moccasin as it is in a leather shoe. As a steel shank cannot be made in the rubber we have put it in the innersole, the value of which cannot be estimated until worn.

Bean's doesn't spend that kind of space on innersoles anymore, not when a single page in their Spring or Fall main catalogs is worth an average of $900,000 in sales. Actually, it ought to be against the law to sell a Maine Hunting Shoe without an arched innersole. The worst ones are the moccasin styles or the lace-up "gum shoes," which will hit the normal human foot right where the heel bones bulge out and cut the hell out of your feet until the bone breaks down the leather rim of the shoe. L.L.'s original, long missing, advice about innersoles is still true: "Every hunter should use them on long tramps. It takes away that flat-footed feeling, making your hunting rubbers feel the same as your everyday shoes." To make his point perfectly clear, Bean added a drawing of a cutaway of a normal shoe showing how the riveted shank is attached to the extension heel and the long counter that also holds up the arch. He also added a cutaway of a leather-top rubber "showing flat sole without steel shank or any arch support whatever. All rubber footwear and moccasins are the same in this respect. They require our Arched Innersole." If you weren't convinced, Bean added medical evidence with a drawing representing an X-ray view of the "Flat Foot (Fallen Arch) Showing result of wearing rubbers or moccasins without Arched Innersole. The entire weight of the body falls dead on the bones, as there is no shank to help support arch. Our Arched Innersole supplies the support needed."

(If you must have a pair of Maine Hunting Shoes to walk the dog, it's still good advice. Bean's increasingly employs people, particularly at holiday time, who may not know as much about innersoles as L.L. did, so you may need the one arcane bit of knowledge required to match the innersole with the boot. Order the same size innersole as boot, except in the case of the wide boot, when you order one size larger. This will improve your opinion of Bean's original invention.)

Of course, Bean was not quite accurate when he said all rubber foot gear lacked any arch support. By 1924 he had added a product that would appear, and disappear, and miraculously reappear from then until today — the canvas and rubber Maine Hiking Shoe, then only $2.90. The popularity of wearing what are essentially high-top basketball sneakers for hiking waxes and wanes, and Bean's usually revives the shoe every ten years. The 1980s model is built by La Crosse Rubber, and was one of the most out-of-stock items in 1981–82, thanks to the modern Bean habit of putting something on the back page without thinking about it. A back-page placement totally disrupts sales projections, probably by subliminal advertising — you toss your Bean catalog on the dresser top and it's 50/50 you're going to be looking at whatever's on the back, even if it's nothing but a tan sneaker.

"While not a heavy shoe," Bean wrote, "the sole is thick enough to protect the feet. . . . Is made of good weight brown canvas with fairly thick pure crepe rubber sole and heel. *It has a steel shank to support the arch, a feature not found in any other rubber sole, canvas shoe.* I have personally given it a thorough try-out and find it the most comfortable shoe I ever wore." It bothered him not that a few pages earlier he had declared steel shanks were incompatible with the construction of rubber-soled footwear. Such mugwumping on the possibility of steel shanks, like most inconsistencies in a Bean catalog, was mitigated by the mixture of enthusiasm and understatement — the soles, after all, were only "fairly thick."

(The current Maine Hiking Shoe does not have a steel arch — an object that really is incompatible with rubber-sole construction. The flexible rubber and the rigid metal eventually go their own ways, and the wearer ends up with a not-quite-dead shoe that has a metal support under the ball of the foot, or slid over to the outside of the arch. Dr. Scholl's once made such a shoe, and I bought them until the company quit making them, not minding at all that they would come unstrung, or unarched, in six months, long before the crepe soles were worn out or the suede leather destroyed. Those of us, including L. L. Bean, who have bad feet will put up with almost anything, and any reasonable expense, to solve the problem, however temporarily. But once the steel shank slips, it is all over, and the shoes are even more uncomfortable than a pair of Maine Hunting Shoes worn without arch-support liners, if that is imaginable.)

The odd-numbered pricing pattern was also fixed by 1926 — only three items in the catalog were sold for even dollars: a pair of socks ($3), the Maine Guide Shirt ($5), and the chestnut brown Bean's Comfort Shoe ($8). The Comfort Shoe is sadly gone from the catalog, and nothing like it is available except at orthopedic shoe stores today. Just a pair of plain old high-tops was the Bean's

Comfort Shoe, and it was clearly, if not explicitly stated, a favorite of the old man's. High-top dress shoes were the standard, of course. If you went downtown to buy shoes, that's what you bought, unless you were going downtown to buy one of those new-fangled things like oxfords. Bean, ever searching for something to clothe his flat feet in, offered the Comfort Shoe, noting that the "present style of footwear makes it next to impossible to get a practical shoe for wide tender feet. There are plenty of wide unsightly shoes that are comfortable," he wrote, fifty years before the brief popularity of the so-called earth shoes — a variety of extremely wide and spectacularly ugly shoes sold to postadolescent hippies in the 1970s. And there were "also lots of stylish shoes that are uncomfortable.

"Bean's Comfort Shoe is made on a combination last having an eight wide ball and a five wide instep with a medium width toe, which not only makes a perfect fitting shoe for wide tender feet [one of the few times that Bean ever repeated himself when writing catalog copy; it was clearly a subject close to the front of his brain] but a very good looking shoe as well. . . . These shoes," he warned, "cannot be fully appreciated until tried on."

The shoes, with their "orthopedic rubber" heels, resemble nothing so much as a mid-cut U.S. Army boot, which was the last comfortable boot the author ever wore, and free at that. But the Comfort Shoe would disappear from the catalog, being, after all, no different from what a Sport could buy at home, if he had a Sport's income and could patronize a reputable shoe store. Bean was learning that that something couldn't just be good, or priced right, it had to be different.

A Fishing Theory
of the Leisure Class

W HEN L. L. Bean discovered that out-of-state license holders would buy his goods sight unseen, he had done much more than invent a marketing strategy — he had inadvertently defined a social group, the Sports, that should not ever be confused with the general run of sports fishermen, deer hunters, trappers and Mainiacs.

Residents of the Eastern Seaboard cities always have provided L. L. Bean with customers far out of proportion to their numbers — to this day, the company's best customers are in New York, Philadelphia, and their suburbs; Boston and its suburbs; followed by the distant West Coast cities, where San Francisco and its suburbs are easily the major market.

The link between the Eastern cities (and the Eastern Establishment) and L. L. Bean is the nonresident sportsman, in Maine jargon, the Sport.

At the turn of the century, three New England states provided New Yorkers (a group that may properly be construed to include anybody in southern Connecticut or northern New Jersey who works in the city) with recreation — Vermont, New Hampshire, and Maine. Vermont (along with its southern appendage, the Berkshire Hills of Massachusetts) provided sedate entertainment — country inns, music festivals, cows, and fly-fishing. New Hampshire provided, in those days before air-conditioning systems, filters, and antihistamine drugs, an escape from city air pollution and common hay fever–causing plants. The vast hotels of New Hampshire — of which Bretton Woods is one of the few still operating, and the most famous, as the home for the post–World War II monetary conference that pegged the world to the U.S. dollar — were populated all summer by families trying to cure asthmas and less life-threatening respiratory illnesses. Hiking in the White Mountains of New Hampshire, traveling from catered "hut" to hut, was coming into vogue. Today's vast army of self-sufficient hikers was yet to be — the Appalachian Mountain Club, with food packed to the cloud-high huts, was typical of that golden age of recreation that lasted until after World War II.

Maine played a third role. It was, from ice-out to the end of the fall hunting season, a place to catch fish, shoot birds, and hunt deer. You can count all the large hotels ever built in Maine on the fingers of your hands, far fewer than in the Mount Washington Valley of New Hampshire at the heyday. Maine was a series of small hunting and fishing camps — scattered out on the vast glacial plain that begins at Sebago Lake near Portland and is stopped only by the Canadian border — the great lakes, Mooshead, Sebago, Aziscoos, Grand, Messalonskee, Parmachenee, Aziscohos, Umbagog, Rangeley, Sebasticook, Meddy-bemps, Millinocket, Millimagassee, Seboeis, Chemquassa-bamticook, Eagle, Square, and Long, and the great northern rivers, the Allagash, the St. John, and the St. Croix, and the downeast Atlantic salmon rivers, the Penobscot, Machias, Narraguagus, Sheepscot, and Pleasant.

There are two kinds of "camps" in Maine, private and sporting. They are neither to be confused with "camping," which either means living in a tent, or going to summer camp. A private camp is a building, ranging from a one-room log cabin with adjacent privy to a twenty-room mansion with central heat and flush toilets, all of it brought in by boat to the shores of a vast, near-wild, lake. The founder of IBM has a camp on East Grand Lake. It is of the latter sort. Innumerable people, most of them residents of Maine, have versions of the one-room, outhoused, camp. In the 1930s, L. L. Bean had nine camps, scattered across Maine from Merrymeeting Bay to Grand Lake Stream. There is, as the Great Chain of Being operates in Maine as well as elsewhere, every conceivable variation in between.

Maine's sporting camps, by and large, are collections of small cabins, increasingly supplied with flush toilets, grouped around a home camp that is the central dining hall, recreation room, and lie-telling arena. Family-style food service predominates, although there are a few camps left that are furnished with college-age waitpersons who insist on being called by their first name.

What was unique about Maine, before the roads penetrated so far into the north woods, what was far different from New Hampshire and Vermont, and certainly the Catskills of New York, was that the sporting visitor to Maine needed a guide — needed a native to take him by hand across the lake and through the rapids and along the portage. In the Catskill Mountains of New York a cult of self-taught independent fly-fishermen developed. They came by train in the nineteenth century, and by automobile in the twentieth. They wrote, and read, a literature on how to catch trout.

In Maine, there has always been a dependence on local knowledge, not book learning. You can read through most of the great classics of American angling with hardly a paragraph in a ream of paper about how to catch fish in Maine — the last great classic, Ray Bergman's *Trout*, is no different than when the literature began in the late 1800s — anecdote after explanation about the fly hatches of the rivers of New York and Vermont, scarcely a word about Maine. In civilized fishing waters, you carried your angler's bible, in Maine, you counted on the guide.

Thus it was that fishermen in the Catskills were just called fishermen, or anglers, and fishermen in Maine were called Sports — it is a we-them distinction, we Mainers and you Sports.

One must remember, after all, that Maine was not a forty-minute jet ride and a rental car away — it was overnight on the train. It was a destination, one not really open to travel in the winter, not a place one got to know. There was no turn-of-the-century grand hotel, no Lake Placid (New York) Club, no Eagle Mountain (New Hampshire) Inn. It was vast and wild and summer-only, in those days.

There is another difference between the Maine sport fisherman and his peers who fish the great trout streams that flow into the Hudson and the Delaware, the rivers that water New York City and Philadelphia. It is complicated, and perhaps difficult to explain to nonfishermen, but worth trying — it is essential to understanding the Sport.

The essence of fishing in the near–New York rivers is the pursuit of the brown trout. From Vermont south and west to Pennsylvania, the quarry is, nine times out of ten, that elusive, wary, finicky-eating import from Europe — often called the German brown trout, though more properly, considering where most of the initial imports came from, the Scottish, or Loch Leven, brown trout. It has, as a fish, a special quality that it shares with another trout —

the rainbow trout of the American West. It is choosy about what it eats. The brown and the rainbow (and transplanted rainbow trout are second only to brown trout in the Vermont-Pennsylvania axis) will eat almost anything — considering the year as a whole — but on any given day of the year, they are likely to eat only one thing. They are creatures of fixation, if not of habit. If they begin the day by eating a small, yellow mayfly, they will not switch until the sun goes down, or they run out of small yellow mayflies. This is what is known, among that garrulous circle of fly-fishermen, as "selective feeding." It is also very boring. What one needs to succeed at catching brown and rainbow trout is a great deal of practical entomological knowledge — all keyed to seasons and water temperatures, and a vast array of artificial flies to match precisely whatever is hatching. I oversimplify the issue, but it would be wrong to go on and on discussing the mental habits of a cold-blooded creature with a smooth brain the size of a green pea.

The well-armed classic trout fisherman does not need a guide. As complicated as fish can be, they can be figured out by competent fishermen, and the details can be explained rather directly, with the use of color prints, line drawings, temperature graphs, and assorted diagrams. This has been going on for years, and a minimal fishing library of truly useful information can be bought today.

Maine, and Maine's sport fish, are quite a different matter. The staple Maine fish is the brook trout. The brook trout is relatively short-lived (a three-year-old is not only fully grown, it's practically senile). Brown trout live at least three times as long, on the average, and there are well-documented cases of twenty-year-old brown trout showing no signs of debility. Because the brook trout is short-lived, it is relatively small. (A very large brook trout weighs

55

five or six pounds, if growing in a lake well-stocked with forage fish. The world's record brown trout is over thirty pounds, lake-bound rainbows have reached forty and fifty pounds.) And because the brook trout is short-lived, it must eat like fury to get up to breeding size and perpetuate itself. It is fair to say that the main problem with catching a brook trout is finding it. Brook trout came to eat. If they are eating small brown flies, it is not particularly difficult to convince them they should eat a large yellow fly with a hook in it. Thus, the problem for the Sport in Maine is precisely local knowledge — where the fish are — as opposed to possession of an advanced degree in troutology.

A person who has been raised on brook trout has very set ideas about how to fish for trout in general, making the mistake that similar names mean similar habits — as a foreign reader of English might, in Mark Twain's analogy, confuse lightning with the lightning bug. A Nova Scotian of my acquaintance, a demon salmon angler and brook trout fisherman, is, to this day, convinced that the rainbow trout is a very interesting fish, but has one strike against it. As he put it, "They're all right, but they won't take the fly." He is happily innocent of the whole literature on matching the hatch of natural flies, he is totally unaware of the whole range of infinitesimal dry flies, not much bigger than a capital *O* on a standard typewriter, which people actually use to catch rainbow trout in the spring creeks when there is a hatch of what is politely called "smut." No, he understands that salmon will not take the fly readily, but he believes all trout are like his native land's brook trout — inifinitely greedy and fond of large red and yellow feathery objects that resemble nothing in nature.

Most Sports regard the brown trout, which is available in a few Maine rivers, as an egregious interloper, and never do find out how hard it is to catch one. Maine's sporting camp customers are not alone in being blessed with the relatively simple-minded brook trout. In the Rocky Mountains and the Sierra Nevadas there is a local equivalent, the cutthroat. A cutthroat (*Salmo clarkii*, named after the explorer) is a small rainbow with a much paler pink stripe and sharp lines of red on the lower edge of its gill covers, lines that stand out sharply against the white throat. Like brook trout, cutthroats can live in very small and tumbling freestone creeks, and feed and grow in extremely cold water. And, like brook trout, they are not particularly fussy about what flies they eat, or when they eat them. About all you have to do to catch a cutthroat is refrain from stepping on it.

The late Fred Pabst, the brewery heir and loyal L. L. Bean customer who popularized the pay-for-play ski area complete with mechanical lifts back in the 1930s, when most folks thought skiing involved walking up the hill first and then sliding down, once was expounding on the virtues of Montana trout fishing to me. "Caught one hundred and forty-three trout one day," he chortled, "and never got off my horse." I said I believed him, and I guessed they were all cutthroats. "Of course they were," he said, "what the hell else would they be?" What else indeed, unless they were brook trout, somehow transported to that country where you can sit a horse at riverside, unlike the overgrown alder thickets that surround almost every Maine stream.

Maine's other great sport fish is the salmon, which comes in two varieties — one is a landlocked version of the Atlantic salmon, and like that Atlantic salmon in open water, will probably eat your lure. For difficulty, it is much like the brook trout — the main problem is finding it. The landlocks move to different parts of the vast lakes as the seasons change, and move up and down in the water, schooling at the comfortable temperatures — sometimes the sun-warmed surface, at other times the icier depths. It is the business of the guide to solve this three-dimensional geographical and hydrographical conundrum.

The sea-run Atlantic salmon of Maine and adjacent Canada is the ultimate fish for Sports. The Atlantic salmon is very large (six to sixty pounds) and very hard to catch. This is easily explained. When the sea-run fish enters a freshwater river, headed back to the place where it first hatched from the egg, it is intent on reproduction. It absolutely does not eat from the second day it enters the river until after it has spawned. Like the reformed smoker who puts a cigarette in his mouth but doesn't light it, the salmon, however, does chew on things. It will mouth a natural fly, or snap at something that looks edible, or else it chews on things that look amusing, or it chews on them because they annoy it. There may be more than three explanations, but it is all perfectly mysterious and you tend to choose the one that fits your mood, the salmon's mood being always impenetrable.

When it comes to catching salmon, the average angler is in absolute need of a guide; he must be part of the we-them syndrome. In fact, the Canadian provinces of Quebec, New Brunswick, Labrador, and Newfoundland have legislated this old necessity into law — only natives are allowed to fish for salmon without paid, professional, advice. Guides not only assist the angler, they amount to a volunteer police force, maintaining the rules of angling on the river.

The special need for the guide in salmon fishing (we speak of the average angler, not the expert) is that not only do salmon not eat on purpose, but they are extremely likely to spend all day in one place, and if you are not fishing over the places where they are lying, you are really wasting your time. Very few Maine salmon rivers have water that you can see through to a depth of more than a few feet, and knowing where the invisible salmon lie is absolutely critical. A decent salmon guide has seen the river at low water, and has a memory of where each and every salmon has been hooked in years past. There are very few decent salmon guides anymore, but that is the fault of the modern age, which has cut mightily into the numbers of natives willing to spend a summer swatting blackflies and catering to Sports, most of whom become fairly disconsolate when face to face with the imperturbable salmon.

The Bean catalog, for many years, insisted that you only need a dozen flies to catch trout, and six to catch Atlantic salmon. It was approximately true. Salmon will eat nothing, or any damned thing, and Maine brook trout can be fooled with fewer than a dozen flies, nine times out of ten. No single sentiment in the history of the catalog indicates any better than the trout fly dictum that L. L. Bean was speaking to the Sport, the Maine-visiting Sport. For the social implications of salmon fishing, and the association of salmon with the L. L. Bean Company, as L.L. would say, see chapter II.

From the late nineteenth century until after World War II, Maine was the exclusive province of the natives — guides and cooks and cleaning women and college kids to serve the meals — and the Easterners who could afford to hire them. It would be impossible to estimate the per capita net worth of the nonresident fishermen, but it is easy to identify them by occupation. They were, to a man, although sometimes they did bring the wife, doctors and lawyers and stockbrokers and businessmen. The angling literature of the era included a number of short stories — John Trainor Foote perhaps the best-read author — on life at the Maine camps, and it was clearly an extension of Park Avenue, Boston's Back Bay, and Greenwich, Connecticut. People went back to the same camps year after year, at the same time of the summer. They were assured of friendly service, yes, but even more, they were assured of eating, drinking, and fishing with people of their same social class. Indeed, the camp was an extension of the club, both of them satisfying that not uncommon human urge to dine among friends, and if not among friends, at least among equals. Trips were planned at the Angler's Club in New York, still vibrantly exclusive and still on Wall Street. By the 1920s and '30s, the Sports were equipping their children in the camp style — hand-sewn loafers and chino pants in good weather, rubber-bottomed boots and down parkas in foul times.

In a way, the simplest definition of a Sport is that he is the father, or the grandfather, of a Preppie.

To this day, the largest possible proportion of L. L. Bean clothing to ordinary gear is seen at a Harvard class reunion picnic, or any given day at Bennington College. That Harvard Square stores offer over fifteen brands (most in garish colors) of rubber-bottomed, leather-topped footwear does not mean that L. L. Bean's Maine Hunting Shoe has been replaced, only that imitation is the sincerest form of social climbing. Bean clothing, with the exception of the chinos and the hand-sewn loafers, was not worn to class at the better preparatory schools until the last few years, when the dress codes ceased to require coat, long-sleeved dress shirt, and tie. For years, the Preppie has been Bean from the waist down, Brooks Brothers and J. Press from the beltline up. But, in the more libertarian private schools, favored by the Eastern Establishment, the Preppie child has been wearing full-scale Bean gear since the 1920s. Mrs. Arthur Schlesinger, Sr., wife of the Harvard historian, recalls her girlhood as a native of Cambridge and a public school pupil, watching the little kids tromping through the snow on their way to the Buckingham School, and the Cambridge School, and the Fayerweather School — instantly identifiable as children of the upper classes "by their little down jackets and back packs and L. L. Bean rubber-bottomed boots that made them look like elves."

Well, everyone looks like an elf, now, when winter comes to Harvard Square and New Haven and Dartmouth and Princeton and Wall Street and the Darien, Connecticut, sanitary landfill. It has long been the assumption that the appeal of L. L. Bean was that it represents the possibility of wilderness, the scent of pine, the rush of bright water. Perhaps it does. The wilderness experience, after all, is expensive. It is distant, it requires leisure time. It is *inconspicuous* consumption, perhaps, but it is only available to the leisure class. And the camp clothing of L. L. Bean represents, as much as a great deal more money spent at Brooks Brothers would, a guarantee that you will be dressed, on some occasion, even if it is only to go to the store, as appropriately as any member of the establishment. Archibald Cox, the U.S. Solicitor General who refused to squelch the Watergate Investigation, drives from his home in Concord to the newspaper store in Wayland, Massachusetts, in his L. L. Bean shirt to buy the Sunday *New York Times*. What more can you ask of a catalog, than that?

L.L.'s Maine:
at the End of the Road

D URING the years that L.L. himself ran Bean's — the
fifty years from just before World War I through
the early 1960s — Maine implanted itself in the mythology of the Eastern sporting establishment in ways that no
other part of the United States ever has, or ever will again.
What is difficult to remember, in this world of automobiles and airplanes, is that Maine managed to keep some
of the reality, and all of the illusion, of wilderness, long
after it had disappeared elsewhere.

The north country's very remoteness saved it from being
overrun, but more than distance made it different from
upstate New York or northern New Hampshire and Vermont. For it was almost entirely privately held, once you
started inland, by the big lumber and paper companies,
Great Northern, International Paper, Seven Isles. Access
to the big woods country, to this day, is at the discretion
of the paper companies, who choose to open their roads,
at their will, to the general public. The Allagash Wilderness Waterway, the federally protected riverway, can be

reached by floatplanes, which fly you to its borders, or over the private roads of the International Paper Company. There is no genuine "public access" to it, and, for many years, that was true of two-thirds of the state of Maine.

Maine resorts and sporting camps were destinations in those years. Side trips taken from them went into the timber company property, or into the only major public area, Baxter State Park. State lands, and all woods, were closed in those years to casual visitors — you could not light an open fire in Maine without a guide's license, a rule encouraged by the paper companies. And so, if you wanted a hot meal, you were required to be a Sport, and hire a guide to keep camp for you. Such a system was unenforceable in the West, but perfectly understood in Maine — one had no intention of roughing it in those days. No one had imagined such things as freeze-dried food and alcohol stoves. There was no interest in the modern fads of light-camping and wilderness survival training and in rock and ice climbing for the sake of the dangers overcome. By the 1920s, when L.L. had the time and money to really indulge himself in hunting, fishing, and camping, a network of state highways and a few paper company service roads had opened most of Maine, and all of Maine that he was interested in seeing. It is no accident that the Bean catalogs of the 1920s and 1930s carried dozens of automobile-related items. The old man's idea of wilderness was an unpaved road, and his idea of solitude was permission to enter paper company property and get away from the ordinary fishermen and hunters who skirted the edges of those baronial woodlands.

The great public access was by water. Maine's lakes were not only places to fish, but also the only chance for the common man to get away from the public roads. But the shores of the lakes and the wooded tributary rivers remained largely private, and spawned the hundreds of small, leased, sporting camps for tourists, and the little villages of modest cabins owned by Mainers, also built on paper company land. Greenville, Maine, on Moosehead Lake, was the primary entry into the north woods — reachable by Central Maine Railroad or tarred state highway, you could rise up the lakes, with a few portages, until you reached the headwaters of the Allagash, and then, via the St. John River, descend to the Atlantic Ocean. Bean had a camp in Greenville proper, and kept a small cabin cruiser on the lake. Although his visits were strictly gasoline-powered, he was recreating in an area which, by the 1920s, had accumulated over sixty years of experience catering to Sports.

The old Sanders store in Greenville, doing business since 1857, was the real outfitter for the region. When people say that they think L. L. Bean, Inc., is a Maine country store, it is a place like Sanders they mean, if they know what they're talking about. They supplied Sports and lumbermen at D. T. Sanders & Son, Co., "with everything needed to camp." Indeed, they were outfitters: "Let us engage your Guides and outfit you with just such goods as are needed for the section [of the country; again, that Maine laconic speech which L. L. Bean had no patent on] at less than city prices." Their advertisements included a letter from a satisfied customer: "I meant to have written you before to tell you how thoroughly satisfactory your provisions were. . . . In particular, your canned peaches and canned peas were the best I have ever eaten." Sanders is still in business, and has all the parts of the L. L. Bean catalog you'd really need, plus homelier items. Cartons of paper plates jostle against a trembling pile of cans of chainsaw bar oil. Life goes on in Greenville out of season, and you can buy a dress shirt or a set of beaver traps in Sanders store. At least one of Sanders' items has been superior to the same offered by Bean — the mandatory red wool crushable hat. The Bean hat had a black leatherette hat band, and if you got insect repellent on it, it dissolved and left you with a black smear across your forehead. Sanders' hatband did not. You would not get away with selling very many dissolving hat bands in Greenville, in black fly season.

When gentlemen went fishing, in the '20s, they wore ties while they were doing it. Bean's inclusion of dress shirts in the catalog was not the least bit quirky. Riffle through the pages of the Bangor & Aroostook Railroad's annual publication *In the Maine Woods*, and look at the photographs — men in ties stand next to guides. Girls have their photographs taken at the top of Mt. Katahdin, wearing middy blouses and skirts. The guides stand slightly to one side, in tan pants and wool shirts and wide-brimmed felt hats.

The sporting camps, most of them well off anything even resembling an automobile road, brought their customers in from the railroad station by horse and team, or by canoe. Kidney Pond Camps, one of the survivors of that era, was reached by train ("Pullman sleeping cars [run] between Boston and Greenville") or by driving from Greenville onto the Great Northern Paper Company woods roads as far as Sourdnahunk Stream, where "our team meets you and takes you to camp." The advertisement made it clear you were on private property, and you would be supervised by the camp, and its guides. A stern warning is attached to the explanation of how to get to Kidney Pond: *NO WALKING*. Other camps were even less accessible — the one on Little Lyford Pond was sixteen miles from the end of the pavement at Kokadjo, near Moosehead Lake, and you came in "seven by motorboat, nine by buckboard."

Little Lyford Camps offered hunting and fishing, and re-assured their guests: "No tubercular patients taken."

That was a promise that carried considerable weight. By the turn of the century, one vast recreational area of the Northeast, one that had been famous for brook trout and black bear and buck deer, was becoming better known as a haven for turbercular patients. The Adirondack Mountains of far northern New York had become a territory of death. The Adirondacks, even before the opening of the sanatoriums, were intrinsically unlike L.L.'s Maine, or the Sport's Maine. "A party of three is about right," L.L. wrote of deer-hunting trips, but in the Adirondacks, three and four hundred hunters would be lodged in five-story buildings, complete with five-story-high gravity toilets so that you not only did not have to go outside, but you didn't even have to go downstairs. Where once these great lodges, the Lake Placid Club, the Adirondac Loj, Paul Smith's, had defined the area as the home of conspicuous consumption in the outdoor life, now the great mountains loomed over tuberculosis sanatoriums. The only known cure was clear air and, on the German model, carefully gradated exercise. Wide paths, meticulously graded to precise inclines — a few hundred meters of two-percent incline, additional leagues of three- and five-percent grades — wound through the grounds of the hospitals. Patients, on rigid schedules prescribed by the doctors, walked, and coughed. Not until the public health services managed to identify and isolate the carriers of tuberculosis would the white plague stop. The Adirondack health industry collapsed during the Great Depression: there were fewer patients, and they had less money for the private sanatoriums. The Adirondacks retreated into obscurity; even the efforts of the Lake Placid Club and the small towns that put on the 1932 Winter Olympics could not quite succeed in making it a destination for the sports-men. Some of the old sanatoriums were converted to prison camps. The villagers shifted from nursing to guarding. Deer hunters and trout fishermen returned, after World War II, but the great age of sportsmanship was over. The automobile was everyman's possession, and the paved roads ran through every valley. There was no need for sporting camps; motels would do.

Maine's destination resorts were almost inaccessible before World War II — located on the big lakes, reached by steamboat from the railhead. Mt. Kineo House on Moose-head, where L.L.'s son Carl preferred to play golf while the old man fished, was twenty miles up the lake, but offered a complete, full-service hotel, separate cottages, a yacht club, the eighteen-hole golf course, croquet, tennis, and "mountain trails which contribute to the complete-ness of the resort." Today, the Mt. Kineo House, like every single full-scale hotel resort in the Maine woods, is out of business. They started to fail in the '50s, and all collapsed in the '60s — the charm was gone, and it was too easy to pack up the car and see more of the country. The farther you got into the woods, the likelier things were to be less spectacular. Up at Square Lake Camps near the Canadian border at Houlton, Maine, the golf course was reduced to "clock golf," but there was still daily mail service (over six miles of water) and, for the nervous Sport, "Radio-phone stock quotations daily."

One could be cynical about the wilderness experience if it means returning to camp at night for stock quotations, lettuce salads, and fresh milk (most of the camps kept their own cows and planted their own gardens), but wilderness for the Boston lawyer was a different concept from the Sierra Club's, it was a wilderness of views and trout fish-ing, not perfect isolation. Even the distant Allagash and

St. John rivers were understood as destinations for sociable groups, not solo trips. L.L. would become familiar with the lower St. John and its tributaries in the 1920s, but not by the rigorous passage from the Allagash. He would drive to it, skirting the big woods, and go salmon fishing far below the howling wilderness. Small parties seemed desolate and forlorn, once on the big river. Sociability, society itself, had to be imported by a critical mass of people. Bean preferred to go by road, and find it ready made.

Warren Moorehead, a Boston professor, writing for the B&A's *In the Maine Woods,* fairly captured the essence of the Eastern view of wilderness, so different than the Western one of great mountains, long vistas, and isolation, and yet, a sense of wilderness beyond L.L.'s capacity to enjoy.

> Eleven of us, in six 20-foot canoes . . . crossed to St. John Pond, a very wild country, and proceeded down St. John stream to Baker Lake. There is no wilder country than that lying about St. John Pond, the head of the river. Here deer can be photographed and nature observed in its wildest aspect. *The stream from St. John Pond to Baker Lake is small, exceedingly wild and very interesting.*

He encouraged visitors not to hurry down the river — "Parties are advised to go up tributary streams, during the journey, and see beaver dams." It is in that sense of small scale, that the wilderness experience was in a view, a photograph of a solitary deer, an afternoon's experience, that characterizes the Sport's wilderness. It was not that you were miles from civilization that mattered, but that you had crossed the boundary from that world into the natural one. And as early as the 1920s, the threat of the intrusion of the other world into the natural one was already felt.

"It is to be regretted on the part of all lovers of the woods that so many macadam roads have been built," the professor wrote. "Real sport in both the Adirondacks and the White Mountains was virtually killed by the advent of thousands of 'week enders' in their automobiles." (A *macadam* road, by the way, was not so loosely used a word in the '20s as it is today. It did not mean a paved road, but, after the plan of the Scot engineer MacAdam, a properly constructed dirt and gravel road with provision for natural drainage.) "Since now Moosehead Lake and adjacent regions are made accessible to autoists," he continued, "it is of vital importance that the upper St. John [that is, the area reached via Moosehead] as well as the Katahdin region, be continued in the future as in the past, natural feeders of game. I am a firm believer in the rights of the general public, but there is such a thing as carrying it too far and this has been done in the West and certain portions of the East. We see the disastrous results." Bean had resolved the problem of easy, pneumatic-tire access and the rights of the public quite easily. Like the bulk of the new generation of Sports, he would rely on the camp and the guide, while the fanatical carried canoes through the fly-haunted portages between Rangeley and the Allagash.

Katahdin was saved, although it has suffered two tremendous forest fires since the 1920s, by Baxter State Park, the largest in Maine and a gift from former governor George Baxter, a Portland Sport who bought it and turned it over to the state. The Allagash section of the upper St. John is also safe, but the professor's fearful comments on the invidious automobile were destined to come to pass in the rest of the big woods.

What is difficult to remember is how recently Maine joined the rest of the world, open to the general public and accessible by automobile. The death knell came in the

1960s. A combination of government regulations and the loss of qualified rivermen stopped the paper companies from driving logs on the great rivers. Everything rolls by truck, now, and hundreds of new roads built into the several million acres parallel the rivers and streams that once carried billions of cords of pulp wood down to the toilet paper and brown bag factories nearer the coast. The paper companies knew that they could not keep the cars out, any more than they had kept out the canoeists. Access is still regulated, often difficult, always over private property and on miserable roads, but the access is there, for the asking. But there was that sixty years, from the invention of the Model T to the end of the river drives, when the greatest part of Maine was all pole, paddle, and portage.

It is not the fault of the paper companies that they opened their roads to the general public. It would have been impossible to keep them closed, certainly to the natives. There is always the problem of what is politely referred to as Allagash Lightning — the disgruntled dropping of a match onto the dry forest floor. The companies have cooperated, under such duress, in opening the woods to weekenders.

The professor's assertion that "the woods about Moosehead" were open to the automobile in the 1920s was a considerable exaggeration, although a road did straggle up the western shore of the lake, and then west to Long Pond and Wood Pond, passing Jackman, Maine, and on to Quebec Province. But it was still largely company land, and river-drive country until after World War II. The first time I went into the big woods, looking for the spirit of L. L. Bean, it was west of Jackman, at Holub Pond. There have been camps near Holub Pond for a hundred years, on the banks of the Moose River. At first there were logging camps and a railroad work gang camp, and then the Sports started leasing camp sites from the Great Northern Paper Company. Until the 1960s, pulp wood was driven down the Moose River into Moosehead Lake, and lumber-sized logs were mule and horse drawn to the tracks and hauled out by railroad — there was not much need for roads you could put a logging truck on, and access to Holub and nearby Attean Pond was strictly by railroad. The Maine Central Railroad, from Bangor to Montreal, cuts through Jackman, on the upper west shore of Moosehead Lake, then by Holub Pond, and across the border into Canada.

Until 1960, one would have come into the Moose River by Maine Central, hitching a ride on the work train from Jackman, the schedule set entirely by the railroad's good offices, subject to its terms. It was on that line, farther northwest, that little Lennie Bean and his cousin caught a ride to the camp where the young L.L. killed his first deer. Now, it is the work of a day to drive up from Boston or Bangor and fish the weekend hours. It is still a fine and wild country, but the fish are not as large as they were in Bean's day, and the deer are scarcer. There is nothing wrong with the water; it is not polluted by the acid rain. It is still good game country, improved by scattered logging operations that bring up the brushy softwoods that deer browse. There are just too many people, it is just too public, for big trout. Weekend hunters are no better or worse than camp hunters who used to come for the season; there are just too many of them. They were good woods to be in, but not great woods. They have, as it were, a slightly used feel to them.

An Aerial Search for L. L. Bean

THERE are still a few corners in the state of Maine where you can recapture the era of Sports, guides, and L. L. Bean. But most of the territory is open to the automobile driver now, and that means the public, and the public is Boy Scouts and Appalachian Mountain Clubbers with their especially good canoes and wandering tribes of teenagers on "adventure weekends" away from their summer camps. And it is also people who fish with worms and wear deer-hunting caps in the middle of July.

The few really private places are way up north in the lumber baronies, and so it was, while looking for the lost world of L. L. Bean, that I agreed to get into a small airplane. (One increasingly admires the editorial abruptness of L. L. Bean, himself. As one might say, copying his style in *Hunting-Fishing and Camping:* persons who are not interested in small airplanes should just read the last three pages of this chapter. People who do not want to know who the most famous man in Maine is can skip those pages, too.)

As a member of the Kitty Hawk Society, whose motto is "Given the choice I will not fly," I did not make the decision lightly. But there was no choice, and it was 9:00 A.M., which pretty much eliminated the second part of the Kitty Hawk credo: "Given no choice, I will not fly sober."

The small airplane was a de Havilland Beaver, a six-passenger Canadian-built aircraft fitted with floats. It was in Greenville, which is more or less the float plane capital of Maine, and it was operated by the oldest flying service in Greenville, which is about as far as I can go with the description because frankly, if you follow me, this is not exactly going to be an advertisement for the company.

What I really wanted to do was get up into the big woods, a long way from the polloi, and catch a three-pound brook trout. This is what you could do, in Bean's heyday, when Maine was a place you got to by train and horse and wagon and pole, paddle and portage. This was what was promised if we got all the way to Fourth Musquacook Lake, which is one of five lakes that lie on Musquacook Stream, which flows into the Allagash Stream. The Allagash is a wilderness area, which means lots of Boy Scouts. But up on Fourth Musquacook, surrounded by the impenetrable woods and logging roads still closed to the public, there would be no Boy Scouts and it would be like the old days. We would fly, but we would get to the very same place, once an old leased sporting camp, where L. L. Bean had come in, via Ashland, Maine, to fish. This is the kind of thing one tells oneself, before getting into a small airplane with floats.

There is, of course, nothing wrong with being a short person. But that is not the same as saying there is nothing wrong with very short airplane pilots. The de Havilland Beaver is a plane designed for pilots more than five feet tall. The pilot was not. That meant, as it turned out, that every time he wanted to look at the ground, he had to bank the plane so he could see out the side window. Also he could not see out the window and look at the floats. The reason a pilot has to look out the window and see the tops of the floats is because there are little retractable wheels, which make the plane, like a frog, amphibious. The very important thing is not to try and alight on water with the wheels down, or on land with the wheels up. During the flight, as the question of the wheels was raised, one began to envy L. L. Bean in his monophibious De Soto.

Usually, you always think, on those rare occasions when you do think about airplanes, that airplanes have lights and buzzers and things to explain to the pilot about whether the wheels are up or down. Not on this one. On this one, the pilot asks somebody sitting in the second seat to look out the window and "tell me if the little yellow things are up." The little yellow things are the pistons that the wheels operate with, and if they are up, then the wheels are up. It would be a hell of a way to tell if you were tall enough to see out the windows.

We flew out, and crossed what in Maine is called "The Height of Land." This is a piece of the old earth that didn't get worn down by the glaciers. It changes the ground elevation from a few hundred feet above sea level to about six hundred feet, not counting the mountains, which are higher.

From time to time the short pilot would roll the plane up on one wing and look out the window, and we would slide around on the seats, except for me, the person with the seat belt on. And after a while, the short pilot said: "Fourth Musquacook, right?" and we said yes, more or less all at once, the four of us, because we were very intent on getting there.

Once you get past Baxter State Park and its centerpiece, Mount Katahdin, Maine gets to be somewhat featureless — or to be precise, featureful, but repetitive. Lots of small lakes. Lots of small streams. Lots of softwood trees, mostly balsam fir and black spruce. No regular roads, just occasional logging roads cut through the timber.

It looked like L. L. Bean country to me, in that there were no McDonald's golden arches, station wagons, swimming pools, or television antennas in sight. And the short pilot said: "Any of you ever been to Fourth Musquacook before?" And one of us said yes. And why? "Because I ain't flown anyone up there for years," he said.

So we got out the map. Lester DeCoster, who was then the northeast representative for the American Forest Industry and who had been to Fourth Musquacook had brought along a map. Lester is a very thorough person who has about as high an opinion of airplanes as anyone is capable of having who has crashed a couple of times while flying over the woods. He doesn't go anywhere without a topographical map, being under the distinct impression that sooner or later, one may have to do some walking. It wasn't a bad map. It was almost good enough to find Fourth Musquacook.

Ordinarily, airplane passengers do not pay any attention to clouds, except that one began to notice that the tops of the mountains were disappearing into what is, I believe, technically known as "ceiling." Ceiling means nothing to someone who is not in an airplane when the tops of the mountains are covered by it. It would have been a word almost totally devoid of emotion or meaning to L.L. in his De Soto.

Eventually we came to a lake that had a camp on it and Mr. DeCoster, who remained a beacon of stability and orderliness through the entire expedition, said it wasn't Fourth Musquacook, but if the short pilot would fly over the camp, he would attempt to identify the location. The camp had a green roof. It also had a flagpole, and on the pole was a flag, and on circling low over the beach in front of the camp, we simultaneously attracted the attention of one man and two Labrador retrievers and determined that it was a state of Maine flag, which made it highly likely that this was, as Mr. DeCoster knew from his wide experience in the north woods, the Maine Forest Service Camp which, if it was, would be on Second Musquacook. So we landed, which made it possible to judge the ceiling, that was now not only covering the tops of the mountains, but their shoulders as well.

"Taxi over and ask the man where we are," at least two of us said more or less in unison and the short pilot did, except he made a little U-turn at the last minute so he didn't have to ask. As a matter of fact, he stared resolutely in the opposite direction while Mr. DeCoster said "Where are we?"

The standard Maine answer, the hardy-har-har response which L. L. Bean admired, would have been: "In a float plane, you damn fool," but we got better service, possibly because we were asking a state employee. "Second Musquacook," he shouted over the noise of the idling engine and the small waves lapping at the aluminum floats on which the little yellow things were thankfully up.

Now, at this point, we all lost our heads, because De-Coster shouted across the water: "Which way is the IP Camp [we were headed for the International Paper camp]?" and the forest service man said, "Two lakes down."

The attentive reader will recall that we knew the following facts before we asked the question: there are five Musquacook lakes. We were at number two. The camp we wanted was on number four. The lakes are numbered sequentially from the one closest to the juncture of Musquacook Stream and the Allagash Stream, and number five is the farthest away. We knew this, but we did not think upon it.

"Two lakes down," Mr. DeCoster told the short pilot, and so we took off and flew downstream. We passed a very large moose that did not look up. It was to be an important moose, but we did not know it at the time. As the Musquacook, like the Allagash, flows from south to north, we were headed north. On reflection, we concluded that the forest service person meant "two lakes down towards Greenville," or "down south." This is the kind of thought you have when the small pilot flips the plane up on one side, points down at the water course below, and says, "I believe that is the Allagash." We all looked at it, including those of us who had not ever seen it. We took a vote. It was the Allagash, we told the short pilot. "So we went the wrong way," someone said, "the man meant two lakes down towards the coast, not downstream."

The small pilot said he would turn around and fly back up the Allagash to Musquacook Stream and then fly right up it to Fourth Musquacook and we said that was a good idea. The pilot did make a U-turn as soon as the valley widened out a little because by now the ceiling was down to the beltline of the mountains and the top of the hills.

We headed south, which is "up" the Allagash, and turned left up the Musquacook Stream, except we did not come to a lake for several miles. This did not make sense, and also we did not see the moose, which was understandable because we had missed Musquacook Stream. It was some other stream. And it stopped in a small lake and that was that and now the directions to fly in were more or less governed by the ceiling. One wished life were as simple in the air as it is on the ground. We would only have to, following Mr. Bean's advice, take out our L. L. Bean waterproof matches and start a small fire, and then take our specially reserved ammunition and fire three shots, the accepted signal for a lost person. Then, warm and safe, we would stay in exactly the same spot and not wander around like chickens with our heads cut off. Unfortunately, in an airplane, one is required to keep moving. At Mr. DeCoster's suggestion, we headed generally northerly, and the back of the short pilot's neck, which was barely visible over the back of his seat, started to turn red. We came to a lake and there was no moose, and no camp. Mr. DeCoster, who was studying his Maine Forest Service Map the way Chinese study wall posters, allowed that it was probably Clear Lake, considering its shape, and we were still south of the Musquacooks, and would the short pilot head a little to the northwest when he got a route between the topless hills? Which he did.

And we saw the moose. One of us alleged that it was the same moose. Mr. DeCoster agreed. That body of water below us was, then, the first Musquacook Lake and therefore we should hang a sharp right and fly upstream, shouldn't we? The short pilot, who had not said a word for almost an hour, turned right, and we went by the forest service camp and the two Labrador retrievers and the forest ranger who stood and stared at us, and onto the third lake and onto the by God fourth lake and the short pilot asked one of us to look out the window and see if the little yellow things were still up, and they were and we landed. The ceiling was down around the middle of the small hills. We pondered our inability to do simple sequential arithmetic of the lake-counting sort.

The short pilot helped unload the baggage, including the three-pound-trout-catching rod. Without a word, he powered up and taxied away from the floating dock and took off into the lowering ceiling, flying back to Greenville in weather I wouldn't fly a kite in.

The camp guide watched him take off and said: "Plenty of room to stay overnight, I don't know why he wouldn't stay and let it lift a little by morning." One of us said that we thought he probably didn't want to sit around and talk about flying, not today, anyhow.

There were, as it turned out, no three-pound brook trout in Fourth Musquacook. The lake had, for years, been famous for large trout, but something had happened, the guide thought, and things were "off." He had once guided L. L. Bean, but couldn't remember much about him, except that he thought L. L. Bean was a fair flycaster: "Not a long line, but smooth."

That was the trip on which I discovered that L. L. Bean was not the most famous man in Maine. We were edging down along the eastern shore of the lake, almost directly across from the camp, when the guide, whose name was Bert, said: "See that big rock?" (I believe I answered "Ayup," being in the habit of unintentionally mimicking the local speech.) "Put a fly right in there, that's where Bud Leavitt caught a five-pounder."

No fish for me by the big rock. That left the barrel hole, which is, or was, the most famous fishing spot on Fourth Musquacook. It was a cold spring hole and once, years ago, there had been a barrel on the shore that marked it. You can find it now by lining up some rocks on the north with the camp on the south, and staying about a hundred feet offshore.

"When the barrel hole was right," Bert said, "which was before they logged that hill up there, which I believe did stop the spring from running so strong, Bud Leavitt took two four-pounders out of there in two casts." Before the trip was over we were reduced to fishing with worms, on the assumption that all five-pound trout dumb enough to eat artificial flies had been caught by Bud Leavitt. We dug the worms in the only kind of place you can dig worms in the north woods, the old kitchen garden of the old, long-since burned, sporting camp that L. L. Bean had visited, there on Fourth Musquacook, very near the Barrel Hole. Digging worms reminds one of the old days. There you are, rooting around the little patch of built-up loamy soil, scrabbling for the descendants of the worms that once cultivated the soil around L. L. Bean's supper.

I had not heard of Bud Leavitt before that trip, but I have since. It came to the point, after several trips into the Maine woods, that the number of places where Bud Leavitt caught a five-pounder, or a four-pounder, and I didn't, numbered in the dozens. For those who come a half-dozen years after him, or sixty years after L. L. Bean, he becomes a sort of Kilroy, that ubiquitous World War II character whose graffiti preceded everyone into the next objective. When we finally met, he corrected Bert's account. "It was a five pound, six ounce, trout," he said.

Bud Leavitt is the sports editor and outdoor columnist of the *Bangor Daily News*, and is, as of this writing, the most famous man in the state of Maine. He has managed to become what L. L. Bean never was, an oracle for residents of the state of Maine. He also became an oracle for certain out-of-state Sports, including Ted Williams, the former baseball player, but that is considerably easier than making it at home.

Bud has been an unfailing source of wisdom, particularly in how to find sporting camps that do not require the use of small airplanes. To travel with him is to be in the presence of a celebrity in towns so small that you would have considerable trouble getting up a softball game.

L. L. Bean was extremely well known in Freeport, but outside of that, he was never much more than somebody who ran a store you couldn't afford to shop at, so far as the state of Maine was concerned. I give one example of the difference between being a cult figure in America, and a celebrity in Maine.

Shortly after the 1970 World Series, when Brooks Robinson of the Baltimore Orioles had starred, and his every move had been chronicled by Curt Gowdy of NBC television, those two showed up in Bangor to film a segment on woodcock hunting for Gowdy's syndicated *American Sportsman* television show. Leavitt, naturally, was the guide. And there they were, sitting in an ABC television van, on a back road north of Bangor, waiting for the technicians to get everything set up.

Curt Gowdy was at the wheel. Brooks Robinson was sitting in the middle, and Leavitt, a smoker, was sitting on the shoulder side of the van, blowing Marlboro smoke out the window, when down the road came a logging truck with an overload of pulp wood, roaring along.

As the truck went by, the driver slammed on the brakes and skidded to a halt, dust flying everywhere. And backed up. And stopped by the van. And the driver looked suspiciously at Gowdy, and stared hard at Brooks Robinson, and then leaned out and yelled:

"Hey! Ain't you Bud Leavitt?"

It is commonly written, and is certainly true, that Bean's loyal customers feel they have a personal relationship with the company, and that when L.L. was alive, a personal relationship with him. That may be true. But Mainers have never had a personal relationship with a company; they have it with people. And since Margaret Chase Smith and Ed Muskie retired from the Senate, it is my best guess that they have it with Bud Leavitt, who represents everything that really matters in life. That is, approximately, deer hunting, trout fishing, and salmon fishing, in that order. Bean's, to them, just means high-priced merchandise. They do not need any fantasies about Maine. They live there.

Merchant's Special: the Salmon of Maine

THE image of L. L. Bean, Inc., at least in those years before women's clothing amounted to half of its annual sales, was inseparably mingled with the Atlantic salmon — a curious fish. There are three reasons for this (there may be more reasons, but when dealing with something as mystical as a company's image, one does well to stick with magic numbers, and the next magic number is nine, which would be stretching things well beyond credibility).

The first relationship is simple. Until restoration efforts (not yet truly successful) began in the 1970s, Maine was the last outpost of Atlantic salmon fishing in the United States — as Montana held the last buffalo not slaughtered by the railroaders and the last grizzly bears not run out of the sheep and cattle ranges of the high Rockies, so Maine was the ultimate repository of that phenomenal genotype, *Salmo salar*, the leaping salmon, but not because, as in the case of Montana, a vast refuge, a Yellowstone National Park, had been set aside for them. Maine's salmon survived because the people had gone away from the hard country where the great fish spawned after arising through the coastal rivers from Bangor to the east.

Salmon everywhere else in the world, from New Brunswick around the rim of the North Atlantic to Spain, have been protected for years by a complicated set of land and water rights that date back to the Middle Ages. In Maine, where they have always been a democratical fish, and any angler may assault them by whatever means are allowed by the state, the salmon survived into the twentieth century because their headwater breeding grounds became less, rather than more, populated from the middle of the nineteenth century into the twentieth. The same population shift to the west that almost eliminated the buffalo meant abandoned farms and tumbled-down mill dams in Maine, particularly north and east of Bangor, where farms reverted to blueberry barrens, and where the great lumbering camps settled down into small logging operations — Paul Bunyan and Babe the blue ox went west, and the headwaters of the salmon rivers — the Penobscot, the Sheepscot (a small river, and the only one southwest of Bangor), the Pleasant, the Dennys, the Narraguagus and the Machias, began to more resemble the late-eighteenth-century Maine woods, with only occasional logging camps, no farms, and dwindling villages.

That is not to say that one could go to Maine intending to catch a salmon, as one might reasonably go to Iceland, or Quebec or Norway. But one could go with hopes of catching a salmon, and hope is everything, in angling.

It is also important to understand that salmon angling has a peculiar magic for millions of people who never intend to try it — I speak of the vast army of trout fishermen. There are millions of trout anglers who have absolutely no interest in catching things like sailfish, or great white sharks, or tuna. The sea does not interest them, they are anglers of bright and moving water, and content with their lot — except, were it possible, they would like to have the salmon. *Salmo salar* is the king of all trout, the archetypal trout, the fish that one would graduate to, if one could. It was a royal fish, legally when there were autocrats, emotionally when there were only democracies. Long extirpated in the rest of the country, more by passageless water-power dams than by pollution — the salmon is more tolerant of pollution than most of its relatives — it gave Maine a special cachet — some miraculousness left over from the days when things were better.

As with many dreams, the reality of Maine's salmon angling was less romantic. Maine's coastal rivers, like much of the peat-bottomed land that lies north into New Brunswick, are dark water, and the few salmon that returned, and escaped the local netters, were in a virtual sanctuary of impenetrable, coffee-colored, water. The first salmon river I ever saw, or fished, was the southernmost, the Sheepscot, and it shared nothing with you but its surface. There is an old farm near the only sensible salmon pool below the very head of the tide, so high that Maine's eleven-foot tides made the river rise but an inch or two, and in the barn of the old farm, high on a shelf, were two or three old gang hooks, weighted trebles made for snagging salmon as the fish rested in the pool nearby. The snagging gear was cobbled together from saltwater cod hooks and plumber's lead. I was shocked then. I am less so now, for although salmon angling is no business for farmers, eating salmon may be.

All the rivers are as dark as the Sheepscot; even the great Penobscot, which rises in clear springs, becomes quite dark before it reaches the sea. Of them all, only the Penobscot is much fished well above tide water — the Pleasant, the

Dennys, and the Narraguagus disappear quickly into impenetrable swamps, the mightier Machias, the northernmost, quickly becomes lost, not only in the uncut woods, but it is impassable to all but the most skilled canoeists, a series of astonishing rapids for so small a river.

For most of this century, fishing was sparse in Maine, perhaps some five hundred fish a year were landed from all its rivers, while the St. John and the Mirimichi, across the border in New Brunswick, would yield thirty thousand salmon a year. It was not much advertised, this Maine fishing. The few camps that specialized in taking Sports to the salmon had enough business, and the hundreds (now dozens) of upriver camps specialized in landlocked salmon and brook trout — fish you could honestly promise to the arriving angler. But Maine's salmon, from the Teddy Roosevelt days until the Franklin Roosevelt days, were nationally known, thanks to the tradition of sending the first bright, sea-run, Penobscot fish to the President of the United States.

This fish was always caught in Brewer, but Bangor got the credit. Brewer is a suburb of Bangor, directly across the river, and the home of the Penobscot Salmon Club, a group of local sportsmen, as opposed to Sports, who maintain a clubhouse high above the river. A salmon, having reached the head of the tide on the Penobscot, is confronted by a low-head power dam, and at least a dozen anglers on the Brewer shoreline. There is a small fishway on the Brewer side, and that, and the natural lie of the river bottom and the flow of the water, has always made the salmon run the Brewer gauntlet, on its way to Washington, D.C. The first Penobscot fish arriving in the capital was a routine staple of the national wire services — the old International News Service, Associated Press, and United Press. The tradition ended in 1937, when a Bangor woman, staunchly Republican, went over to Brewer and bought the first salmon, announcing quite publicly that she was not going to have a respectable Maine fish sent down to that "communist" in the White House. The tradition was never revived, even with the election of Eisenhower — and never will be. The old low-head dam is crumbling rapidly, and the first salmon is just as likely to be caught on the Bangor side of the river, or well above the dam, far from the sanctity of the Penobscot Salmon Club's home waters. Such traditions cannot be maintained without a social network, and the first-fish angler is often, these days, a nonmember.

The regulations on the Penobscot are standard ones, and include injunctions against fishing close to the fishladders, a series of artificial pools like stairways, with concrete risers and waterfilled treads, that allow the fish to pass over the dams step by step. About fifteen years before I heard the word Penobscot, I had heard of Bangor. Mort Sahl, the original intellectual comedian, returned to San Francisco from a tour of the nation's less-likely nightclubs. He'd been to Bangor, Maine, he said, and he asked a cab driver where the action was — so, "he took me to this place where they fish illegally." They still fish illegally in Bangor, much to the dismay of game wardens, fishermen, and reporters. A few years ago I wrote a newspaper article which suggested that the regal salmon had an ennobling effect on the anglers who pursued it. Local and visiting anglers were complimented for their civility, generosity, and sportsmanship. A week after the column ran, they arrested fifty-eight people in Bangor for assaulting salmon in closed waters and attacking them with clubs, spears, gaffs, nets, and ganghooks. What had happened, as it turned out, was that an unusually hot and dry spring had turned the Penobscot into a warm-water spa, and the salmon, desperate for cold water, had turned up some of the small tributaries, including the cold brook that runs smack through the middle of downtown Bangor. This brought the salmon to the attention of large numbers of genuine Maine wood-burners, which is this decade's sobriquet for the semi-poor who try to eke out a living without steady work in that inhospitable climate. The presence of fair numbers of large fish brought out the worst in these modern-day hunter-gatherers. While these folks were not salmon anglers in the true sense of the word, I am also beginning to have my doubts about the morally uplifting qualities of the fish on dedicated fly-fishermen.

Whole sections of the lower Penobscot have attracted a crowd of regulars, mostly paper mill workers with night shifts, who essentially hog the bank, keeping casual visitors away from the salmon. There is, of course, no solution for these problems in a democracy except social disapproval. The sensitivity of paper mill workers to peer pressure is evidently not great, and at last view, they were still hanging on to their stretch of bank just below the old low-dam fishway, with all the tenacity of a Scottish laird whose deed to the water had been registered with James the Sixth and First. Up on the Machias and the Narraguagus, a few locals have managed to make themselves unpopular, not by hogging the bank, but by adopting an air of possessiveness and secrecy about which fly is working, or which pool is holding fish, that would offend any general sensibility. What becomes clear, after consideration, is that salmon anglers, as a class, are indistinguishable from the same number of persons selected at random from the telephone book, with rare exceptions. They are all fanatical, and if they are also obnoxious, devotedly obnoxious.

The second relationship between salmon and Bean's is

quite direct. If the President's first-fish kept reminding the nation that Maine had salmon, L. L. Bean did the same for his customers, routinely carrying a selection of Atlantic salmon flies ("six patterns are all you need") and occasional references to his own success. *Hunting-Fishing and Camping* shows the patriarch with his "record" catch from the Plaster Rock pool on the Tobique, a tributary of the St. John in New Brunswick, and the picture was reprinted in *My Story:*

"Taking five salmon in a single day, L. L. Bean of Freeport Saturday broke the record for the famous Plaster Rock pool. . . . Mr. Bean . . . set another unusual record by taking each fish on a different pattern of salmon fly." No wonder he thought six patterns would suffice.

When it came to salmon angling, L.L. was a Sport himself, depending on leased water and guides for his sport. At deer hunting and grouse shooting and waterfowling, he remained a country boy, gunning with his friends, including some madcap grouse shooting around Freeport with George Soule, the manufacturer of Bean's Best Decoys. But in moving to salmon angling, L.L. was changing from catering to Sports to being one himself, and the relationship between the social class of Sports and Atlantic salmon angling is so close as to be a definition of the word Sport. That is the third relationship in the triangle of Maine-Bean-Sport.

A vice-president of L. L. Bean, Inc., recently remarked that even if the duck decoys in the catalog weren't paying their way, "we have to keep them, we can't sell those ladies' dresses without them." If duck decoys mean "outdoors" to customers (and they certainly mean "outdoors" to department store window dressers, who can hardly put a tweed jacket in the window without a faded, chipped decoy nestling in the corner), it is salmon flies that mean outdoors to the upper classes in the Eastern megalopolis.

First of all, salmon angling is anglophiliac, it is the sport of British royalty and British gentry. Second, it is expensive. It is perhaps the only truly expensive thing you can do without giving the appearance of conspicuous consumption — even if you are paying $2,000 a week for the fishing rights to an Icelandic river, you are still dressed in wool shirts and rubber waders — Eastern yachtsmen may dress down with worn deck shoes and faded shorts, but they are still sitting on a quarter of a million dollars' worth of yacht. But salmon fishermen are, well, just fishing.

The apogee of Sportism is membership in a club that owns fishing rights, and if, for example, the St. Botolph men's club in Boston has three hundred members, it has but two members who belong to a good salmon club in New Brunswick. One belongs to the Black Creek Club, the other to the Salmon Brook Club, and the ratio of 150 to 1 is an appropriate measure of the relative difficulty, and status, of the two memberships.

The second tier of Sport is obliged to patronize salmon camps, which are commercial establishments that sell weekly packages of food, shelter, guiding, and salmon pools. These camps are patronized by real Sports who were so unfortunate as to not inherit a salmon club membership, and by would-be Sports, such as the author, who occasionally wastes his money on salmon angling. One, for instance, will occasionally encounter an insurance salesman, or an orthodontist, at a commercial camp, but one encounters insurance company presidents and medical doctors in the salmon clubs. Pseudo-Sports are easily distinguished from the real thing by speech, by concern about such trivia as the food, and by the fact that they have new-looking fishing vests, and don't know the names of the guides.

There is also what is known as public water — all of Nova Scotia (the least productive of all the Maritime provinces' salmon fisheries) and Maine are public. As democratic leanings (not to say socialistic movements) increase in New Brunswick and especially in Quebec Province, more and more water is repurchased or confiscated from its absentee owners, and opened to the public. By and large, you cannot define the public water fisherman — he is sometimes the purest of Sports, less often a pseudo-Sport, and most often just the Public, both foreign and domestic. Since New Brunswick and Quebec require nonresidents to hire a guide, even while fishing public water, the presumption is that we are therefore sports, with a lower-case s, even if not of that social class of upper-case Sports.

It would be a mistake to focus too much on the expense of salmon angling as the essential ingredient that makes it the very definition of a Sport. There is a subtler, technical reason. In all of North America, and in the more respectable waters of Europe, one is legally, or socially, required to angle with the artificial fly. Fly-fishing-only waters are often set aside for trout anglers, but the salmon is protected, as a species, wherever you find it. To say that you have been salmon fishing is to say that you have been fly-fishing, a recognizably superior form of angling, but you say it without having to spell it out. It is, of course, the essence of upper-class behavior to make something perfectly clear without actually saying it.

It is true that most gentlemen angle for trout with the artificial fly because it is neater, and more fun, than angling with worms. (Virtually all female trout anglers use the fly, as their social status on the river is already suspect enough without being caught with a box of worms. My aunt was the only exception to this rule I ever met. She always fished with live grasshoppers, but not very seriously. She was utterly indifferent to any one else's opinion of her, in any case.) But not everyone who choses to fly-fish does so for the best of reasons — there are times when nothing else will work. In the later part of spring, and the summer, when the trout have been feeding on natural flies, they regard worms as suspicious objects and ignore them determinedly.

Salmon are quite the opposite. Since they do not eat once they enter fresh water, they strike at the artificial fly for no apparent reason. They are much likelier to mouth, if not swallow, something juicy. They can be driven by anger to striking a metal lure, if it is held right in front of their noses. I recall watching four British gentlemen angling for salmon in the fly-fishing-only waters of the House of Dun on the South Esk River, near Montrose, Scotland. One of them was dangling a fresh shrimp (that is called "prawning"), the second was heaving a large metallic lure with a spinning rod, the third was drifting a hook adorned with six angleworms, and the fourth was standing out in the open, fly-fishing, where he could be seen by, and see coming, the river warden. This was quite shocking, I thought, not so much from the salmon's point of view as from the social point of view. They were, after all, on a salmon fishing holiday, and all of their friends and relations assumed they were fly-fishing.

The reader may be thinking, at this point, that the writer has a less-than-glamorous opinion of the Sport. This is not true; they are very much like the normal run of people, except with more money. Salmon angling is not likely to bring out the best in people, as it tends to reward them almost randomly. Catching a salmon is a chance encounter, more often than not, between the fish and the man. Those people who can afford the most time at the river with the most salmon will catch the most fish. For the rest of us, those of us who are standing next to a deranged salmon will catch it, those of us who are standing next to normal, noneating, nonbiting salmon will not.

On rare occasions, it brings out the very best in an angler to confront this fish, as in the case of the Doctor Who Fished the Narraguagus. He is what a Sport should be, or could be, if it were a better world.

The Prince of Sports

SALMON angling, under the circumstances available to most of us, might best be described as considerable repetitive behavior in anticipation of extraordinarily infrequent, capricious, and unpredictable rewards, or as they call them at college, "reinforcements." The psychologist B. F. Skinner discovered this rule of animal behavior back in the 1930s, and several generations of graduate students have taught pigeons to peck at button "A" tens of thousands of times before getting their randomly returned dab of bird food. In Maine, the place where the largest amount of effort was expended for the least frequent reward of salmon was, for decades, the Cable Pool on the Narraguagus River in Cherryfield.

The only consolation I ever got there was meeting the doctor, and that has made all the difference. It is sometimes too easy to sniggle at the Eastern Establishment, the Sports and the Preppies, and to forget that their values, if imperfectly expressed by most individuals, are still real and attractive. The doctor who fished for salmon was a customer of L. L. Bean, and otherwise a perfect example of his kind, but more. The more is what this chapter is about.

The Narraguagus rises up in the blueberry barrens, where few if any salmon are ever caught, at least legally. It flows over a modern dam erected in the 1950s to save the residents of Cherryfield from the consequences of their folly in building homes on the floodplain, then through the Cable Pool, the Railroad Pool under the Bangor and Aroostook bridge, the Maples, the Academy Pool across the street from the abandoned high school, down to the Salt Water Pool, just below the head of the tide. Cherryfield is east of the glitter of Acadia National Park and Bar Harbor, summer home to the Rockefellers and their ilk. The only industry is the Stewart Blueberry cannery, and after the salmon fishing is over, in the heat of the summer, the Indians come down to rake blueberries. In June and July, there is nothing but the fishing.

Bud Leavitt, as I mentioned, the most famous man in Maine, and I drove up from Bangor and pulled in at the Cable Pool. The name comes from a U.S. Geological Survey station. The cable allows someone to ride a small car out over the middle of the river and measure its height, a matter of no interest to anyone as long as it is not in their cellars. The steel cable cuts directly across the middle of the pool, and, by mid-July, is usually festooned with short pieces of nylon fishing leader and an assortment of whatever salmon flies anglers are using that year. It is by far the most popular pool, the last pool before the ascending salmon reach sanctuary at the fish ladder over the flood-control dam, the place where the few fish that enter the Narraguagus each year will rest the longest before traversing the dam and disappearing upstream into the barrens. At the pool, there is a small gazebo with racks for fishing rods under the roof, a few picnic tables, and a pair of benches for telling lies. The racks for the rods are part of the culture of the Cable Pool, they are numbered from 1 to 24, and you make your reservation to fish down the pool by putting your rod in the last unoccupied spot. You are then free to sit on the bench, or wander downstream, past the painted rock that marks the socially accepted lower limit of the pool, and fish down toward the Railroad Pool with your spare rod, while waiting for your number to come up at the Cable.

I elected to fish down, and the Most Famous Man in Maine chose to sit on the bench. We would have at least a two-hour wait before it was our turn to pass the thousandth fly of the week over the alleged salmon that lurked in the coffee-brown water. The Cable Pool is a taking pool. If you are not a salmon angler, I should explain that a taking pool is not just a place where the fish stop, but a place where they will stop and, while there, take the fly. Salmon stop many places, they take the fly in fewer. The most famous nontaking pool in North America is the Cains River Bridge Pool on the Mirimichi (it is the bridge to get to the Cains River, but not on that stream). In the poorest of seasons, you can walk out on the bridge and see a half-dozen salmon lolling next to the bridge piers, but you cannot catch them. They are a sort of advertisement for the place, and as untouchable as a Playboy Bunny.

There is a bit of the Cable Pool that can be covered honestly by standing just below the painted rock and casting upstream, and then there are a series of pockets, slick water below the rocks, as the river tumbles down to the small Railroad Pool. After not catching a fish in the lower Cable, I started to not catch fish while moving down through the pockets, until I came up behind a man who was fishing very well, and very far off, dropping a large brown deerhair fly — something like a rat-faced Mc-Dougall — on a pocket more than halfway across the river, perhaps eighty feet away. That does not sound like a great distance if you have been believing everything you read in the outdoors magazines, but the average fly-fisherman has considerable difficulty throwing a line from one horseshoe stake to the other, a mere forty feet, with any consistency. You can test that sometime, if you happen to stay in a proper Maine sporting camp, which has horseshoe courts by definition.

I stood below him, out of the way of his upstream arm and his backcast, and watched him drop the fly, just across the slick water, and then pull it back quickly, dropping it with some slack so that the fly would float for a few seconds on the flat water before the sidecurrents snatched it out of the break and carried it downstream. And I remarked, when he stopped and reeled in his line, that I did not know you could catch salmon that way, it was a good trick for trout lying below a rock, but I did not know that the more deliberate salmon would manage to find the fly. I am afraid that is the way fishermen introduce themselves more often than not, by talking too much about fishing.

He said it worked, sometimes, and we introduced ourselves. He did not refer to himself as "doctor." The only salmon-fishing doctor who ever introduced himself that way on the Narraguagus turned out to be an optician, and a grouchy son-of-a-bitch at that. The doctor was from near Boston, and I asked him if he fished the Narraguagus often, and he said he did. It turned out, I found out later, that he had fished it every year since 1928, the year he graduated from Harvard Medical School, and only missed a couple of years while he was in the service during World War II, even then managing a train ride up from Boston on a weekend pass one July. He had caught his first salmon in the Narraguagus and, I believe, his last, fifty-six years later.

And then he asked me if I would try his salmon rod and tell him if I thought it was as nicely put together as he did. I have had a lot of Sports show me their fishing rod and tell me how good it was, or expensive, or rare, or specially made to their own design, but most men are as honestly interested in your opinion of their fishing equipment as they are in your opinion of their wife, or their toothbrushes. It was a nice rod, fiberglass with a little graphite added (Lami-Glas "S" if you would like to have your own), and it had a most relaxed action, not soft, or wishy-washy, but refined and casual. My own rods tend to be too powerful for their own good, a sort of overstatement of what a flyrod should be — I buy them thus to compensate for my own inadequacies.

So I expressed my real admiration for his moderately priced flyrod, and we chatted amicably, and fished on down toward the bridge, taking turns with the small pockets (to be honest, taking turns with the small pockets within sixty feet of our bank, for, once I joined him, the doctor stopped working the more distant pockets). I asked him if he had a rod in the waiting line up at the Cable, and he said he did not, that he didn't usually fish it if it were crowded and people were waiting so long for their turns.

"It wasn't always so popular," he remarked, stopping to light his pipe. "I found it, you know. No one knew it was there.

"Before the war, before the dam was built of course, we fished up above the Cable, right where the dam is now. It was called the Cold Water Pool, because of the springs in it. One day, I don't remember why, I decided to fish down through where the Cable is now. It was all alders and overgrown, and you had to wade right down through it. It must have been low water.

"Well, the sum of it was, I caught two fish and lost two more. Imagine that, and no one knew it was there, that it was a taking pool."

What the doctor did, after he found the pool, was what almost no other salmon angler in the world would have done. He went down into Cherryfield and told everybody. The very same day. Within that season, they had cut down the alders and opened the pool up to fishing. It had no name for years, until they put in the water-gauging station, and the cable-car. By rights it should be the Doctor's Pool, but not everything happens by rights in salmon angling.

I saw him a few more times. We were always planning to go duck hunting, but things were never quite right, particularly in the matter of having enough ducks and not too much ice on the marsh, and so we only saw each other on the river, once every other year or so, when our trips overlapped. I heard about him, occasionally, from the Most Famous Man in Maine, or someone else. One day, down at the Bangor Pool, Maine's chief salmon biologist came into the clubhouse with astonishing news:

"Someone caught a salmon up on the Narraguagus and released it."

He thought it had been the first time since at least 1950 that anyone had actually turned a fish back on purpose. And, no, he didn't know who had done it. This was of great interest to Famous Man, who made a telephone call to the local biologist up in Cherryfield. It was the doctor who had caught the fish and astounded the onlookers by quietly slipping it back into the river. Those who knew him better were not surprised.

I had a drink with him the last year he went up to the

river, in his room over at the motel on Route 1. He wasn't drinking anymore, not that he ever had a problem with drinking, but age had taken the enjoyment out of it, and, I believe, it made his heart flutter a little bit more than it already did. It was his whiskey, of course, as the mere fact that he wasn't enjoying it anymore didn't mean he shouldn't have some in the room for friends who stopped by. We could have had dinner together. He said he would like to, if I didn't mind the food in the motel restaurant. We didn't. I wanted to drive back to Bangor, and even in those long July evenings, I would get there after dark. I had not yet given up whiskey, I told him, but I had given up doing much driving after dark; it was tiring. And that was all right, he said, although, I think now, it wasn't.

We talked a little more, all of it about fishing, but not about catching fish. There is a great deal more to fishing than catching fish, once you fall in love with it. He had caught salmon in many places, but it seemed necessary to him to come back to the Narraguagus (I don't believe I ever heard him refer to the river, as many anglers do, as the 'Guagus) because it was important for him to see how the river was doing, from year to year. He had invested in it, or fallen in love with it, and he was not a person given to random affections.

The last thing we talked about was the difference between fresh and saltwater fishing. He did very little of the latter, although he was born and raised in a coastal town. Oh, he had enjoyed it as a boy, he said — dropping handlines off the baithouse pier in the harbor. But one day, he heard someone talking about trout, and he asked his father, who ran a dairy farm north of Boston, if there were trout there. His father supposed there were. And how do you catch them? His father supposed you could use a worm.

So he cut an ash sprout for a pole and took some hand-line and a hook and some worms, and went trout fishing. You could not find the brook now, he said, it is behind the dam of the town reservoir, buried under the still water. And he went creeping up to the edge of the brook, at a likely place, and dapped the worm down onto the water, and caught a trout. He had never seen such a thing, a brook trout, all red spots and flaring white gill covers and the red and white front fins.

"I suppose that did it. I fell in love with bright water, with moving water, and lost all interest in sea-fishing."

He was, I think, the best Sport I ever met. And he was one, with his L. L. Bean chamois cloth shirts and his pull-on, low-cut, Maine Hunting Shoes and chino pants. But he wore them with ease, and the Sport's uniform is as difficult to wear with true unaffectation as a tuxedo, or any costume.

The Most Famous Man and I were discussing the doctor one evening, the pair of us a long way from home. We talked about the discovery, and the immediate disclosure, of the taking pool below the Cold Water Pool. One of us remembered the story about him releasing the salmon back into the Narraguagus, the first modern, if not the purely first such event. I mentioned the bourbon, kept on hand in case of social necessity.

"They do not make gentlemen like that anymore," the Famous One said. "You and I are not like that and we never can be. The world has changed, and the possibility of being like him is gone. Who did you ever meet, except him, who always gave more than he took?"

I said I knew a couple of people who are working on it, as best they could in these parlous times, but I thought he was right. There is only one Narraguagus, one Cable Pool, one doctor. That is all we get, though we might spend a lifetime looking for another.

L.L.Bean
Fall

Prose and Products: the Curious Mind of L. L. Bean

I F it is true that the prose style of the Bean catalog in- dicated, by its pure idiosyncrasy, that there was a real person hiding in the pages, the old product line, the real Bean line, was even greater proof. Today's catalog grows harder and harder to tell from the competition's — if Or- vis has British moleskin trousers, Bean's will have them a few years later. If Land's End markets lightweight air- plane-style luggage, so will Bean's and Orvis. And Orvis and Land's End copy Bean's original product line — rub- ber-bottom, leather-top shoes; chamois cloth shirts, cot- ton sweaters. Not so when the old man ran the place, and for the very good reason that when he was running it, he was already an old man, set in his ways, and convinced of his own genius.

The prose could have been a deliberate construction, a parody of country directness, but the product line was palpable, visible, proof that someone of great individual- ity was running the store. Consider, for example, Bean's Duck Hunting Coat, which, as we have noted, was not for hunting ducks, but made out of a wax-filled cotton duck fabric. It has hardly changed in sixty years, and was the first thing like it in the history of hunting. Until Bean decided to make his own, people went hunting in almost anything, depending on the conditions, but typically in work clothes. Very few Sports did much serious bird shooting in Maine, because partridge hunting is far removed from the gentlemanly sports of pheasant hunting or quail hunting. Pheasants are shot, the world over, in fairly open country, particularly grain fields. Quail, even in the brier-infested American South, tend to be hunted in open meadows and the edges of plowed fields, and gentlemen hired guides with dogs, and the dogs did the hard work.

But Maine hunting, for partridge and woodcock, is one long grim encounter with brambles and briers and wild rose and hawthorn with inch-long thorns and alders still dripping with morning dew or melting frost, and Bean invented the nearly perfect garment when he hit on wax-filled duck cloth and roomy pockets. In the Maine woods, you do not have someone handy to carry your game for you, or a buckboard to carry the lunches to the field.

Bean tried, after he added a rubberized rear pocket to hold dead birds, to figure out a better way to get the bird from hand to pocket, and for a few years marketed a Duck Hunting Coat with a "tunnel" pocket that opened in the front, allowing you to push the bird from your belly around to your backside. That was abandoned, after several years, because the tunnel opening was constantly catching on thorns and twigs. One of the things that is a necessity, in a grouse woods, is sometimes just bulling your way through the underbrush, belly-first. The tunnel pocket is occasionally revived by other manufacturers, but it has no utility in the real woods.

A man who had invented the Maine Hunting Shoe and

the Maine Duck Hunting Coat might properly regard himself as a first-rate inventor, and Bean did, although that was really the end of it, as far as objects of any great utility were concerned. He would tinker with the Duck Hunting Coat, adding ventilation under the armpits one year, putting full flaps over the pockets another time. As he got older, he went for the little comforts, including a little piece of cloth-backed sandpaper stitched to the inside, for he was having increasing difficulty, at the age of sixty-plus, lighting matches in the woods.

As Bean himself grew more sedentary in the late 1930s and 1940s, products began to appear that were directly related to the creature comforts of someone who was starting to do most of his fishing and hunting from a seated position. He designed a Cold Proof Duck Hunting Coat with a full sheepskin lining and extra-long sheepskin cuffs that could be turned down to make hand muffs. And that could be topped off with a "roomy garment designed especially for duck hunting," a parka made out of wool "Camp Blanket" material. You'd weigh a ton, dry, with all that on, and if you fell in you'd need a derrick to get out of the mud, but, after all, there comes a point in life when staying warm is half the battle.

He invented some things, and remained a sucker for apparently ingenious inventions of others. While sensible "car campers" were already using the Coleman line of white gas lanterns and stoves, Bean fell for a competitor's product, and offered it in 1933 as "Bean's New Instant-Lighting Stove." What made it light instantly, compared to the somewhat crankier Colemans, where you had to heat up the coil of white gas until it vaporized before getting a pressured gas to the burner, was the Bean stove burned "gasoline easily taken from your car tank." (That was true in the '30s — gasoline was sold under such poor conditions that draining out dirty gas through standard pet-cocks in the tank was something every driver knew how to do. Men knew how to patch innertubes, too, those days.) Gasoline, of course, is one of the most explosive liquids known, but, one would have to agree, "instant-lighting," and burning leaded gasoline under the hotdogs would have added spice to the whole procedure. Other car camping items were added from year to year — vacuum bottle sets, and "Bean's Compartment Grill Plates," which were paper plates, something you would have trouble recognizing unless you knew something about the paper mill business, but honestly described as: "Manufactured for us from State of Maine new spruce logs and thoroughly sterilized dur-ing every process of manufacture. Everyone who . . . en-joys picnics should own a quantity of these plates." They were introduced in 1942 — replacing the aluminum plates Bean had carried since the 1920s, as aluminum was then restricted to wartime use.

After inventing the Maine Hunting Shoe, Bean couldn't let well enough alone, and started stitching lightweight all-leather, rubber-soled, moccasin bottoms to them and called it the Leather Top Moccasin — "the result of many months' experimentings to perfect a shoe that can be rebuilt the same as we rebuild our Hunting Shoe" so that when "the bottom part is worn out we can attach new bottoms as shown below for $3.50 post paid." And even that was not enough: "After wearing out the bottoms of our Leather Top Moccasin, you can," Bean gloated, "if you wish, have us attach our Hunting Rubber. . . . In other words, you can use our Leather Top Moccasins until snow comes and then have our Hunting Rubbers attached for $2.85. Again in the Spring you can have them changed back to Moc-casins." That program lasted a few years, and then Bean gave up, and started selling a more durable moccasin-style boot. The problem with the leather-top on leather-bottom moccasin was that it took the disadvantage of the Maine Hunting Shoe construction — a complete sewn seam from the toe, all the way around the ankle and back, a necessity for attaching the rubber bottoms — and imposed that problem on a standard leather shoe style.

Bean could "invent" anything to keep the ladies busy at the sewing machines. A drawstring bag became a "Slipper Bag — Made from fine brown 10-ounce duck. Instantly closed or opened by double-action puckering string. When on fishing, camping or business trips protect your clothes from soiled slippers by using this inexpensive bag. (30 cents, postpaid)." As early as 1930, Bean had discovered the virtues of assuming that most of his customers were businessmen who could carry his stuff along on business trips, and introduced the Bean's Brief Case, the same handleless model still sold. "A very roomy case," he announced, perhaps thinking of all businessmen as salesmen, as were the ones he met daily, "that will hold order books, catalogs and small samples."

He had added the oxford cloth shirts by 1932, on the assumption that you needed something nice while traveling to and from camp, but the illusion that it was an outdoors item was frequently dropped. He announced, without explanation, that "Every outdoor sportsman needs collar attached shirts. Ours are made from the finest grade fully shrunk oxford cloth we can buy." He sold a twilled broadcloth blue- or tan-striped shirt that was a classic Eastern college button-down as "Soft, comfortable, dressy," and then, almost as an afterthought, "For dress or sports." He sold Hathaway dress shirts as "semi-dress shirts," again with the note they would be "something out of the ordinary to wear going and coming on their outing trips." Indeed, even the illusion began to break down. In 1943 he offered Bean's "Business Man" Oxford; Almost apologetically, he wrote:

"Primarily manufacturers of hunting and fishing supplies, we do not have a regular so-called dress shoe in our line. However, our 'Business Man' Shirt has gone over so big we decided to list this very popular 'Business Man' Oxford." It was made of smooth calfskin, much more than "so-called" dressy.

The quirky little additives to standard items were Bean's forte — of the drawstring "Maine Duffle Bag" he wrote, "There is nothing better for packing dunnage into auto, buckboard or canoe," and he claimed to have added a personal touch: the "Strong loop on bottom as shown for tying bag on running board." (It occurs to me that there may be readers who do not know what a running board is — it was a thing like a shelf that ran from the front fender to the back fender, underneath the car doors.) He created "Bean's Bird Shooting Cap" of duck material with a "genuine leather visor," like a baseball cap — but he made one with double visors, back and front, "that gives complete protection from sun and rain $1.25." The all-leather Duck Hunting Cap (as opposed to the hat made from duck) was offered only in the single-billed version, but was "100% perfect as to color, shape and general make-up for duck shooting. *When slightly soiled it blends almost perfectly with the general surroundings of duck marsh.*" You could, however, get another of his creations, the "Bean's Leather Hat," a full two-inch brim that came "also in plain olive green for duck hunting."

There were items of Bean's manufacture that probably did not make themselves well understood to the nonhunter, as the "Blood-Proof Game Bag, Made from heavy waterproof slicker cloth for carrying game, liver, or lunch." It is common practice, when dressing deer in the woods, to bring the liver back, leaving the carcass in the woods until you can round up some help to carry out, or drag out, the deer. Carrying out the deer was the source of one of the old man's strangest inventions, a folding stretcher with a bicycle wheel mounted at one end, handles at the other — intended, once you figured out how to get a two-hundred-pound deer up on the stretcher, to allow you to push your deer out of the woods as if it were on a wheelbarrow. "Saving you the price of hiring a horse, and deer look much better when not dragged." You, of course, have never seen a one-wheel wheelbarrow on a bicycle-sized sixteen-inch wheel — it puts the center of gravity up much too high, and it wants to tip sideways and wrench the handles out of your hands — but Bean had a few built and kept them in the catalog for a dozen years.

Bean hated to allow anyone else's name into the catalog, and for many years, only the Hudson Bay Blanket was acknowledged, and that only after the Hudson's Bay Company threatened to sue him for using their name without permission. He ended up buying the blankets, and the right to use the name, from the company. One of the rare instances of using another name occurred for two brief years, 1933 and 1934, when he offered "Darton's Duck and Goose Straps." In those days, you could hunt over live decoys, and the duck and goose straps were little devices to go around the live decoy's foot, attach the duck to the anchor, and keep it swimming in front of the duck blind. But, if he had to sell Darton's by name, he could always offer "Bean's Improved Duck Strap" which was "the same as the Darton Strap except it is only about one half as long . . . [and] made so light and short it can be left on leg the entire season without the slightest discomfort or injury to the decoy. One person can put out Decoys faster than two can using the old style strap and with less danger of bird getting loose." Two years after Bean offered the duck straps for the first time, the U.S. Fish and Wildlife Service outlawed the use of live decoys as one of several measures to protect the rapidly declining wild populations.

What we will never know, except for a hint, is what L.L. invented that never made the catalog. At a testimonial dinner for the old man, Fred Goldrup broke up the crowd with a brief reference to one of L.L.'s crankier creations. Goldrup, who was Bean's first employee — he stitched the leather tops onto the first Maine Hunting Shoes — was asked if L.L. ever made a mistake. Yes, Goldrup said, he made one good mistake when he decided the trouble with rubber rainwear was it kept tearing on things, so it would be more sensible to make rubber underwear. Bean's Best Rubber Union Suit was an unqualified disaster.

Fishing brought out the best, or worst, in the old man, as it does in most anglers — any gimmick will be tried. He did not care much about the actual quality of the basic rods and reels and lines he sold (and the company never did, until the late 1970s, and then with some disastrous results as they tried to enter the high-priced market). Most of his equipment was standard, middle-of-the-road quality. His split bamboo rods were not even up to minimal standards, and he acknowledged it: "Makes a good rod for the beginner, also for the experienced fly fishermen who take along a spare." But he did like gimmicks: Bean's Transparent Nature Bait ("many fishermen claim this Bait is more effective than live bait"); he brought out a natural-looking mayfly using "a new waterproof silk wing . . . that makes it the most durable and most lifelike of any fly we make." Perhaps his finest moment was the cobbling up of the Bean's Minnow Bucket. He took a standard "cricket cage," a galvanized wire device for holding "frogs, grasshoppers, etc.," and sewed a canvas water bucket to hold the cricket cage: "When used for minnows the cage is placed inside the bucket to serve as a form. Bucket is practically waterproof up three quarters of the way. From this point the water gradually oozes out just fast enough to keep the water cool and fresh three times as long as a metal pail." But, if that didn't work, you could always buy Bean's Indestructible Rubber Minnow.

Invention in fishing matters was sometimes a matter of emptying out your pockets, as with Bean's Brook Trout Flies: "We have made a survey of hundreds of brook trout flies to determine how many we could eliminate. We have decided that nine flies in two sizes are all that are necessary, and in many cases four or five will answer nicely." (For landlocked salmon, "Have decided that 12 flies in two sizes are all that are necessary and in many cases 4 or 5 will answer nicely." Atlantic sea-run salmon, a most mysterious fish in any case, required further research: "We sent a questionnaire to a number of our customers who do a lot of fly fishing for Salmon. From their replies we decided that six flies were enough." (For salmon fishermen's interest, Bean listed them in order of their effectiveness: Silver Doctor, Jock Scott, Black Dose, Dusty Miller, Silver Grey, and Durham Ranger.)

When one considers the New Bean and the Old Bean, clearly what is missing so particularly these days is the quirky, foolish item. The product line was always mixed, women's and men's, street wear and woods wear, and, if the New Bean is heavily devoted to trendy women's clothing, even L.L. himself was not a purist. After he married his second wife, a registered nurse, in 1941, he carried white nurse's shoes for several years. But what is gone, along with the inimitable prose, is the sheer variety of small and meaningless and idiosyncratic items. There is no inventiveness in the New Bean, no sense that someone who reads *Popular Mechanics* and fishes is sitting up late cobbling up a two-billed cap or a cheap minnow bucket. There is not that aura of authentic dabbling that L.L. had. He, and he alone, could get away with buying Dr. Grabow's patented pipe, available in every drugstore in North America, and labeling it "Bean's Moisture Proof Pipe." Only he could take Edgeworth Pipe Tobacco, and repackage it as "Bean's Special Pipe Tobacco." They were, and are, fine, low-cost products, but outside of the ambience of the Bean catalog, not something you needed to send away to Maine for.

Bean's success at mail order spawned some half-dozen rival enterprises in the 1930s, including one based seven miles down toward Portland, the R. C. Nichols Corporation of Yarmouth. It was the closest thing to a Bean clone, and included a four-color cover with sporting scenes for spring and fall, and an attempt, eventually unsuccessful, to imitate the Bean principles. The Nichols catalog suggests what happens to imitators of pure originals — they are often doomed to failure.

What good was it to print a picture of the owner, Ray C. Nichols, and promise that "all orders received and filled . . . come under the personal supervision of RAY NICHOLS whose one aim is to manufacture and sell only superior quality goods," if the language lacks that essential, quirky spark? Nichols sold a zipper duffel bag (for fifty cents less) that was identical in every detail to Bean's, except better made, with heavier leather handles and thirteen-ounce instead of eleven-ounce duck material. But L.L. wrote, "This is our idea of the handiest duffle bag that can be made. . . . With most duffle bags it is necessary to dump all the contents to find a pair of stockings or a box of shells." Ray Nichols could only point out that the zipper opening "makes it convenient for inserting or removing articles." No contest.

Nichols made a leather, handleless briefcase that superficially resembled Bean's Brief Case. Mr. Nichols tried the personal touch "Designed for my personal use," but didn't notice the real difference between his and Bean's and didn't point it out. The L. L. Bean case was eleven inches deep and fifteen inches long, on the outside dimension, which meant that standard legal-sized yellow pads wouldn't fit in it, as the sewing and the seams at the end made it about fourteen and three-quarter inches on the inside dimension. The Nichols Utility Brief Case was fifteen and a half inches long, overall, and held a legal pad. To this day, the ordinary Bean's Brief Case is still a fraction of an inch too small, and you have to order the legal size, which is, well, oversized.

Both Bean and Nichols bought pack baskets from the Penobscot Indians, and resold them. Bean's was made by a "Tribe of State of Maine Indians who have earned their living by basket making for the last century." Nichols's was simply "of Indian manufacture by a Tribe of Maine Indians." But, on inspection, the Nichols basket was a superior product, with half again as many rows of woven ash, cut in slimmer pieces. Nichols's "four peck" basket was of forty-five withes, compared to about thirty for Bean's similarly sized basket. And if Nichols said his "Basket is safe container for carrying breakables," Bean was much firmer: "The Pack Basket is the only safe container for carrying breakable goods."

Nichols was yards ahead of Bean on one count — he had stock numbers for each of his items, while L.L., until his death, made no use of item numbers in his catalog. And, like Bean, Nichols tried to emphasize the 100-percent money-back guarantee — "Every piece of merchandize

Nichols' sells is guaranteed to be exactly as represented. If any article does not measure up to this guarantee we invite your comments." But L.L., as usual, was more direct: printed on the edge of his 1930s-era order form was the guarantee, translated into the customer's point of view: "It is understood that if not pleased in every way with goods ordered, I am to return them at once and receive my money back. *It is also understood that I am not required to give any explanation or excuses for returning them.*"

The 100-percent guarantee was nothing special in 1930s mail order. Farther down east in Bangor, the Wight's Company, a purveyor of trapping gear — everything from animal scents to twenty varieties of animal traps — tried to horn in on Bean's business for a few years — and unlike Nichols, Wight's took him on right in the heart of his business, with a copy of the Maine Hunting Shoe, Wight's Maine Hunting Boots, of which Mr. Freeman L. Wight wrote: "I have worn a pair of these boots for the past two seasons [in 1935] and can tell you they are the most satisfactory I ever had." Wight's even cloned off the Rubber Moccasin, and a version of Bean's Duck Hunting Coat. They stopped short of copying the Bean's Business Man's Shirt, but would offer Wight's Hand Made Neckties of garish design. "Individualistic," Mr. Wight described them. "No one in your town will have ties like these."

And after a few years, no one, anywhere, had Mr. Wight's ties. Bean rolled on, and the local competitors dropped by the wayside. After a while, there was only one Bean, just as there was only one state of Maine.

Everything You Could Possibly Want to Know about the Maine Hunting Shoe in One Long Chapter

To say that L. L. Bean manufactures the Maine Hunting Shoe is to exaggerate the importance of what goes on in Freeport. The company stitches four pieces of leather together to make the upper, and attaches it to the rubber bottom. The actual value added is less than 10 percent of the cost of the boot.

The manufacturing ingenuity and the material and labor costs are two thousand miles west in La Crosse, Wisconsin, where the rubber bottoms are assembled. La Crosse lies at that meridian of the Midwest where the land begins to break and roll along the Mississippi, where mountains appear possible again after a thousand miles of prairie. It is exactly at that intersection of north and south where, if someone says their favorite sport is skiing, they could mean water skiing or real skiing.

There are three major industries in La Crosse, a city of ninety thousand with the highest per capita income in the Midwest. The world's largest brewery, Heileman's, looms on a low bluff near the Mississippi River above the Chicago, Burlington, and Quincy railroad yards. Trane, the giant air-conditioning company, sprawls across the eastern edge of town, and just behind the Trane factory rises the block-square gray wooden hulk of the La Crosse Rubber Mills, where the Maine Hunting Shoe begins.

The manufacture of rubber goods is little changed since L. L. Bean had the cobbler sew a pair of galoshes onto leather uppers. Should there be a 1918 rubber mill employee reincarnated today, he could go back to work at La Crosse tomorrow suffering only the jet-lag of metempsychosis. There would be no changes inside the plant as profound as on the street outside — there is no rubber manufacturing equivalent of the automobile.

The Hunting Shoe is thus singularly archaic, both in manufacturing technique and in raw materials. It is largely made of real rubber, of the stuff gathered in the jungle.

Rubber is nothing but dried sap, and as with all vegetable substances, it is susceptible to rot. There are half a dozen ways to preserve it, all similar to the techniques used to preserve food. You can merely dry it, and it will not molder so rapidly. You can use common salt, as is done with North Atlantic codfish, creating those boards of indestructible protein. You can mix it with a variety of bacteria-killing chemicals. The dark brown rubber that Bean's specifies for the Hunting Shoe uppers is processed in the oldest, and still the most satisfactory, manner. It is smoked, like a Smithfield ham.

A generation ago, the uppers were made of 100-percent natural rubber, the stuff known in the trade as Number One Smoked, the most expensive, pure, and flexible of all the grades of jungle rubber. The stock for Bean uppers is half synthetic rubber now, and more expensive to manufacture. Number One Smoked, gathered, dried, and cured by hand half the world away from La

Crosse, is less than half the cost of synthetic rubber, 44 cents a pound for the best Thailand smoked compared to nearly a dollar a pound for the artificial stuff turned out of petrochemical factories a few hundred miles down the Mississippi. The increasing use of synthetic rubber was forced on the mill by that ubiquitous culprit, air pollution.

Ozone, the chemically active molecule of oxygen (O^3, rather than the benign, ordinary O^2) is produced naturally by lightning bolts and the action of sunlight on the sweet exhalations of trees. That is what Spiro Agnew and Ronald Reagan meant when they said trees cause pollution. Whales, of course, go to the bathroom in the ocean. It is a question of understanding the proportions of the problem. Ozone is produced artificially by electric motors, and the reaction of sunlight with the dank breath of automobiles, trucks, and power plants. The ozone capitals of the United States are Los Angeles and Denver. Los Angeles has more automobile emissions, but mile-high Denver has more ultraviolet light.

For the uppers, La Crosse mixes, by volume, 50 percent Number One Smoked with two synthetics: 30 percent EPDN, an ozone-resistant synthetic, and 20 percent of a man-made rubber that closely parallels the molecular structure of natural latex. The beauty of Number One Smoked is its extraordinary lightness and the great length of the molecules — but the long thin and elastic molecules are perfect prey for the oxidizing ozone, which cuts them into shorter and shorter chunks, and after a few years visible cracks appear in pure rubber. The EPDN is all short and thick molecules, amoeboid rather than filamentous. Though ozone cannot cut it so quickly, EPDN has two curses — it is twice as heavy as natural rubber, and with short molecules, it cracks quickly from repeated flexing;

like the proverbial rope of sand its particles are too small to braid together. The synthetic imitation of Number One Smoked mediates the mixture of natural and artificial. It has longer molecules than EPDN, shorter ones than natural. The Hunting Shoe upper is, then, a compromise, and inferior in use to the one you could have bought when there were more horses than people in Colorado. It is not so light and flexible as the original, and in spite of the efforts of chemistry, will not last as long as it used to. In this case, the fault is in the air, not in the underlings that make the product, and the original, all-latex upper would disintegrate after a year in Los Angeles, or a couple of winters sitting in the basement next to the electric motor that drives the oil burner.

Raw rubber, as it sits on the loading dock, is one of the most intractable substances in the world. Even the best smoked rubber is tacky to the touch, there is a certain beastlike quality to the bales, they are irregular and sloppily cut, and tend to mold themselves around any obstruction — a pillar, say — if the day is warm. So it will be through the entire manufacturing process. To spend a day in a rubber footwear mill is to understand why so much of what once was made of light and flexible rubber is now manufactured, more easily, from stiff and heavy plastic.

The first step in milling rubber is to chop it into fist-sized chunks and heat it and stir it until it flows together into five-hundred-pound batches of what looks like brown bubble gum. The next problem is to chew it, as you must chew bubble gum, until it is workable. As with curing and preserving the rubber by smoking, the technology is another adaptation of food preparation. The Cuisinart that grinds the bales up into workable chunks is a Banbury mixer, named after the small town in England where they were perfected. Chewing the rubber into a workable state is done on pairs of polished steel rollers. It is almost exactly the same process as making noodles. The rubber is squeezed through the wringers repeatedly until it is thoroughly mixed and elasticized. The difference between a rubber roller (a calender, from the Greek root whence we get cylinder, and pronounced with the hard *c* of the original *kylindros*) and a pasta roller is more one of size than purpose, but the difference between rubber and pasta dough is as the difference between lightning and the lightning bug. The rubber is tended, cut off the calender, folded, reinserted between the slowly turning rollers by hand. As with everything else done to rubber, there is a minimum of automation. Vast bubbles form in the folded rubber and they pop explosively. It is the sound of gum snapping, at well over 95 decibels.

Mr. Goodyear's invention, the vulcanizing process, as every schoolboy once knew, involves adding sulfur to the raw rubber and then heating it to around 300 degrees Fahrenheit. Sulfur is mixed as soon as the raw rubber exits the Banbury mixers, and then the rubber must be kept workably warm, but not warm enough for vulcanization to begin, until the product is completed. The sulfur is added on the calenders, not inside the mixers, where it would cling to the sides of the machinery. By the calenders that front the mouths of the Banburys, there are dozens of aluminum doggy dishes, each holding a pile of bright yellow sulfur. It is simply sprinkled on the rotating rubber and gradually, over thirty minutes of calendering, blended into the dough.

Calender technology predates rubber manufacture by several hundred years — not only in pasta machines, but in cloth and paper manufacture. British worsted wool was calendered on wooden cylinders in the fourteenth century, paper since the sixteenth. But using the calender as a mixer, rather than a finisher, is unique to rubber goods.

It is at this point in the manufacturing process where modernity disappears — the massive machinery and the complex mixture of synthetic and natural rubber, with additional chemicals to speed the vulcanizing process, some clay to give it substance, and a smattering of artificial coloring agents, gives way to a series of largely un-mechanized hand operations. Unfinished rubber is, of all the substances man tries to shape, the most intractable. In a word, it is sticky.

A number of sticky things are made in factories, but the stickum is added at the last moment — as with fly paper. In a rubber mill, the yielding, tacky material goes through every step of cutting, shaping, pressing, and molding in the parlous state that it exits the calender rollers. Along-side every cutting machine, piles of scrap rubber accumulate — pieces not cut exactly to pattern, and the left-overs. Within minutes the piles of scrap begin to weld together — what once was a multitude of delicate pieces of rubber each an eighth of an inch thick becomes a solid mass. And this would happen to every bit of rubber in the plant if it were left in contact with its fellows for a few moments. The solution is as old as pastrymaking, and as tedious.

Rubber squeezed to the right thickness on finishing cal-enders is rolled up by hand, with a strip of paper pastry cloth between the layers. Once cut to shape, the individual pieces — boot uppers, boot soles, or any of the half-dozen other parts of the Maine Hunting Shoe — are picked off the cutting line by hand and placed on trays. The wood-framed trays have twenty pieces of cotton canvas pastry cloth bound to one edge — these are "books" and a leaf of cloth is turned over each layer as it is covered with cut rubber. Material-handling technology in the rubber mill consists of nothing more than carts of books and carts of rolled-up rubber, pushed by hand from station to station.

If it is the curse of rubber that it sticks to itself, so it is also the blessing — products like the Hunting Shoe have no glue in them at all, and no stitching except where the leather uppers attach to the bottoms. They are small monoliths of latex — they derive their strength not from the separate ingredients, but from the homogeneous elasticity, as with the head of the sperm whale.

Boot bottoms are built inside out and upside down on inverted aluminum lasts — most of it is done by women. One after another, they reach for a piece of stock, picking the components one at a time off the leaves of the books. The first one puts on the inner sole — fabric coated on one side with rubber. The fabric side goes down on the last, it will be the side that goes against your foot. The next woman tops the innersole with a layer of sponge rubber to cushion your step, and a third laminates the sponge to the innersole with a layer of double rubber-coated fabric. The next drops a stiffener, made of chopped-up rag and rubber, usually just the ground and calendered leftovers of single- and double-coated cloth. The stiffener is smaller than the double-coated fabric, and it leaves a border around the edge of the sole — this will mark the line, and leave the space, to attach the uppers. Small pieces of double-coated fabric — called "friction" — are added at the toe and heel for additional strength. So far six people have worked on assembling the shoe, and eighteen more have been involved in cutting and booking the components. The two parts of the upper, the vamp that goes over the ball of the foot and the quarter that wraps around the heel, are pressed onto the last — two more women to assemble, and six to cut and book the parts.

The basic tool for welding the rubber parts together is a stitcher — a phrase adapted from leather footwear manufacturing — but a rubber stitcher is just a small hand tool with a smooth end for pressing the tacky rubber tightly together. So far, thirty-two women have literally had a hand in making the rubber shoe bottom, as each of the eight pieces has been picked off the cutting machine, booked, and assembled by hand. Robots can do a lot, but robots don't do sticky.

The final step is the toughest. The heart of the Maine Hunting Shoe is the chain-tread patterned yellow rubber sole that wraps up around the insole to the brown rubber vamp. Every other part of the boot is die-cut, with machines that are ubiquitous in the footwear and cookie industries. The chain-tread sole must be cut one at a time with a mechanical knife because it is a beveled cut, tapering up and out from the chain-tread design so that when it is wrapped onto the upper, it tapers neatly into the rest of the boot. Cutting the soles, stamping the size, attaching the heels and bringing them to the assembly line requires five more hand operations. Forty-one people and counting. One woman presses the completed outersole onto the last. Forty-two.

Stitching the outersole to the uppers is not only men's work, it's young men's work. Their right arms are twice the diameter of their reasonably muscular left arms, and they are crouched over the lasted boot bottoms, forcing the boot soles to meld with the uppers, using roller-tipped stitchers to amalgamate the two pieces of rubber. Counting the two dozen men it takes to calender the rubber and bring it to the cutting areas, the forty-two women involved in cutting, booking, and assembling the uppers and soles, and the final stitching by men, sixty-five people have prepared the boot bottoms for the vulcanizing ovens.

Vulcanizing, the process that Goodyear discovered by accidentally dropping a mixture of sulfur and rubber on a hot cookstove, is done today in steam ovens. Most rubber goods are vulcanized in a mixture of steam and gaseous ammonia, but not Bean's shoe bottoms — ammonia darkens rubber, and the uppers would turn nearly black, the yellow soles nearly brown. An hour at 270 degrees of pure steam cures the material. Stripping the lasts is the final hand operation. Like every other job in the factory, it's paid as piece work, and the urge to make money collides with the need to let the aluminum lasts cool enough to strip the shoe without burning your hands. The men who strip the lasts have bare hands that look like leather gloves.

La Crosse Rubber Mill can crank out about 2,500 pairs of Bean bottoms a day — annual production is a company secret, but it is probably near capacity, a half-million pairs a year.

Bean's also has captured most of the rest of La Crosse's mill capacity. When they reintroduced their canvas hiking shoe, they had it built at La Crosse. After putting the canvas shoe on the rear cover of the 1982 spring catalogue, orders boomed, and now the only La Crosse canvas and rubber shoe made in the United States is the Bean hiker. Everything else, including La Crosse's old trademark shoe, the white-soled, blue canvas oxford, is imported now.

The leather for the Maine Hunting Shoes come from a tannery less than a hundred miles north of La Crosse, on the west bank of the Mississippi at Red Wing, Minnesota. S. B. Foote, still family-owned after all these years, is the country's largest producer of high-quality boot leathers, and the town is a center for work shoe and boot manufacturing.

Modern chemical leather tanning is an odd mixture of

high technology and hand work, of antique processes and computer-driven quality controls. In the nineteenth century, when a Maine farmer expected to cobble his own work shoes, he made at least one pair a summer. He had no hope that the bark-tanned leather would last much more than a year.

Almost all modern leather goods are made by the single-bath chrome tanning method. Although Bean still advertises some "elk-tanned" leather goods, they are neither elk, nor treated with any parts of an elk. It is just a color, and a phrase that hints at something mysteriously outdoorsy.

Tanning can be thought of as a three-stage process, although the actual number of steps in producing a hide for Bean's is numbered in the dozens. Hides are cleaned of everything not wanted, the remaining fibers are chemically altered, and the final finish restores some measure of suppleness and waterproofing. Essentially, the leather has to be stripped of life and then reincarnated as a flexible, breathing, sterile material.

Americans specialize in cow and steer hide because this is beef country. Calfskin for Bean's fancy dress loafers is imported from Britain, while all the heavy leather they buy is of American manufacture, the final by-product of our hamburger culture. It might seem romantic, or practical, to make boot leather out of tough old steers off the rangeland. We tend to think that a rough existence will turn out a tougher hide, but age and hard living conditions do nothing to improve the inherent qualities of a piece of cowhide. Old hides are almost useless for boot leather. The interior of a hide is a mixture of fibers and undifferentiated material — protofibers. In the older animal, as in the older human, that plump interior weakens and disappears. We get wrinkles, and cowhides turn into porous fibrosities. The most waterproof leather of all is made from calfskin, but it lacks the thickness required for boots. Tanners pay premium prices for the skins of cattle that have spent their entire, short life in feedlots — there are no brand marks, barbed-wire cuts, or coyote nips to mar the leather and increase the proportion of waste.

Hides arrive in Red Wing by truck, Herefords and Holsteins mostly, red and white, black and white. Although as flat as cartoon characters after the steam roller passes, they remain recognizably cattle, hair and all. They've been salted at the meat packer's yard, and doused with insecticides, and they smell like dead mice in the wall.

Tanneries are divided neatly in two parts — wet side and dry side. The wet side is all bad odors, dangerous chemicals, and water, the dry side is all clean smells and oil. Leather moves through the tannery from the ground up — from receiving docks and washing areas to the elevated floors where more delicate operations take place. Drafts of air coming up elevator shafts and stairways are frequent reminders that there is a ground floor laden with old parts of young animals.

Loosely speaking, the purpose of the wet-side processing is getting rid of everything that isn't leather, including hair, dirt, flesh, fat, and biodegradable proteins. There is no "skin" on leather; the superficial cluster of cells that we think of as skin and might call epidermis if we were talking fancy has to come off the hide. It is a matter of great convenience to the tanner that the layer of "skin" cells includes the base of the hairs. It dips down into the hide, surrounding the bulb of the hair. It is almost miraculous that the protein that makes up the fiber and protofiber of the hide, what will be the leather, is of the class of collagens, and the epidermal layer is all keratin, because the superficial layer of keratin is destroyed easily by bacteria and by caustic chemicals.

Historically, the keratin, and the hair it surrounded under the skin, was removed entirely by bacterial action. The neighborhood of a tannery resembled the interior of a dead skunk, so much so that in the nineteenth century it was common to separate the process of preparing the skin for tanning from the factory where the final tanning occurred. The relegation of tanners to the inferior castes in Buddhist countries is usually ascribed to religious motives, but the very nature of the work would be enough without the more complicated analysis of theologians. Putrefaction, while it removed the skin and hair from the hide, could continue on until it had destroyed the interior fiber. This was stopped, and still is stopped in such tourist attractions as the environs of Marrakesh, by adding other substances, including pigeon dung and human urine.

The modern method, which is substantially more acceptable to the neighbors, is to attack the keratin with lime (calcium hydroxide) and other chemicals. Still, there is a small amount of putrefaction going on in the vast wooden vats, certain bacteria being able to survive in the strongly alkaline solution. (Human beings use chemicals in a similar way — the liquids used to slough dead skin off the human foot are mild caustics that erode keratins.)

Liming is followed by bating — neutralizing the action of the lime, dissolving a few odd classes of internal proteins, and firming the hide. This was the stage that once required large quantities of pigeon and chicken dung, but now uses ammonium sulfate and a few peculiar protein-dissolving enzymes that are extracted from cow innards. Hides fresh from liming are, understandably, puffy and soft, waterlogged and stretchable. The bating process is straightforward enough — ammonium sulfate is analogous to the contents of a shaver's styptic pencil. Both are varieties of alum, the astringent that clots blood and puckers the skin shut. What the flabby hides need is massive puckering, and they get it in the bating baths.

Tanning, historically, depended on a class of vegetable compounds — tannins — that furthered the puckering-up and coagulating of the protofibers deep inside the hide. Human beings hardly ever encounter vegetable-tanned leather in the twentieth century, and our commonest association with tannin itself is in red wine. It is the tannin in red wines that gives them that astringent, that puckering, quality when they are too young in the bottle. It is also the preserving effect, the natural antibacterial action of grape tannin, that makes reds the longest-lived of wines. The stems of grapes are high in tannin, though not so high as the old leather industry's sources — oak, hemlock, sumac. The highest concentration of natural tannin is in the leaf galls of oak trees, and collecting them as they dropped in the fall was a source of income for small boys and girls through the nineteenth century.

Vegetable tanning survived well into the nineteenth century, and was doomed as much by the problems of modern life as anything inherent in the process. The fundamental problem with vegetable-tanned leather is that it breaks down in the presence of extreme heat — any temperature over 150 or 160 Fahrenheit begins to destroy the congealed fibers. Such modern workplace conditions as boiling water, steam, the heat of foundry and factory floors would soften it, eventually destroy it. Stories of marooned explorers boiling and eating their boots and animal harness were at least possible as late as the nineteenth century — even more so if the leathers were tanned by that other commonplace method, which used cod liver oil as the primary tanning agent.

Of all the chemical methods devised in the nineteenth century, one has survived, so-called chrome tanning. A dissolved salt, essentially chromium carbonate, is used to congeal the protofiber and sterilize the interior of the leather. The chromium is blue in solution, and the wet side of a modern tannery is an endless chain of pale blue hides moving from bath to bath, and into the final washing drums.

The smells end with the tanning process and the final washing. The hides tumble clean in rotating drums the size of cement truck barrels and emerge in a state of cleanliness that seems impossible if you remember what they looked like on the truck, what they smelled like in the bating tanks. Once, soaked to the waist by the splash of water from an emptying drum, I expected to have to change clothes and shower. But in a few hours, the water had dried, and there was not a hint of odor, nor a visible stain. I would not have expected so happy a result if it had been plain tap water.

The washed hides are stretched and plastered onto metal panels and sent down a continuous line through slow drying ovens, peeled off the frames, shaved to a standard thickness, and repeatedly oiled and passed through calenders to squeeze the oil through to the center of the leather. It is called "stuffing," this oil-and-roller process, and it is the final process before the leather leaves the Mississippi and moves to Freeport. There is nothing particularly magical about L. L. Bean leather — equal and better grades stay home, moving across town to the Red Wing Boot Company, or moving a few miles downstream to the Russell Moccasin Company, or across the state to Gokey's, the latter two companies being America's last bootmakers to routinely manufacture custom-fitted footwear.

The Maine contribution to the Bean Hunting Shoe was that onetime inspiration of L.L.'s — that perverse, and initially unsuccessful one, of sewing rubber bottoms to leather tops.

Fame Comes to Freeport

*L*IFE magazine was the first national publication to take notice of L. L. Bean (which was not surprising, since Time-Life publisher Henry Luce was a Bean customer, like many a Yale man) with a photographic essay on Bean's products in their "Life Style" section. But October 13, 1941, was hardly the time to make a killing in the mail-order business, with the war going on in Europe and Pearl Harbor just seven weeks away. The rest of the *Life* issue indicates a country gearing up for war, not the outdoors. Even ordinary consumer items, like automobile spark plugs, were advertised as being necessary to military success, in PT boats or Jeeps.

Bean, who never lost the ability to count a dollar, wrote that the *Life* magazine "four-page 'write-up' . . . was a big help to our mail order business. One full page showed pictures, descriptions and prices of nineteen different items from our catalog. *To have bought this space would have cost us about $48,000.*"

Indeed, the *Life* piece was pure puffery that you couldn't

buy for love or money, including pictures, and prices, of thirteen pieces of clothing, the complete line of Maine Hunting Shoes and eighteen different knives (but not the famous jelly spreader). "Laboratory tests may be good enough for city slickers," the *Life* writer sneered, "but Mr. Bean prefers the endorsement of a Freeport resident who has given tough wear to a shirt, sock, . . . or machete." But the business just sputtered along through the war years, presumably to grow and thrive afterwards.

L. L. Bean returned to the national consciousness in 1946, a year marked by as much hope for an outdoor recreation boom as any in American history. The rush of returning veterans, the revival of the domestic automobile industry, the urge to forget the war, made the nation's industries, and publications, outdoor conscious. It was the *Saturday Evening Post* that discovered L. L. Bean, but it could have been any of the national magazines.

The postwar boomerism infected more than publishers — one of the most spectacular investments in anticipated outdoor sporting expenditures was made by the Republic Aircraft Company, one of many wartime industries looking for a way to capitalize on their manufacturing capacity in the face of a peacetime economy. Republic developed a two-passenger amphibious airplane, the Seabee, specifically designed for the flying fisherman — the cockpit door opened forward, and the angler could shut down the engine, stand up, and start casting as soon as the ripples had died. They priced the Seabee at about $6,000, and sold some six hundred before it became increasingly obvious that the number of flying fishermen had been greatly exaggerated. Tooling up to build the Seabee had cost Republic more than $12 million when, as they say, a dollar was a dollar. Grumman Aircraft, a company that already made amphibians, managed to sell a few of their smallest plane, the Widgeon, to sportsmen, but what little market there was for pilot-owned amphibians was grabbed by the standard airplane companies who fitted their production models with factory-designed, and Federal Aviation Agency–approved, floats. Grumman did take its surplus stock of aluminum, and its naval-architecture expertise gleaned from building flying boats, and turn to the production of aluminum canoes — the Grumman canoe became what the seaplane could never be, the ordinary man's way of getting away from it all.

The *Post* article appeared on December 14, 1946. It was not well timed to increase Bean's sales. It appeared, he noted, "between the mail order seasons, and at the end of the Christmas buying," but it did produce inquiries and requests for catalogs, "which are the basis of anticipated mail order business." In fact, nothing except news of the old man's death in February 1967, carried on all the national networks and in most of the national magazines, would ever produce so many inquiries in so short a time. The *Post* article brought in nearly thirty thousand letters in the last two weeks of December and the first two weeks of January 1947. Bean's demise was good for fifty thousand inquiries in the February and March of 1967.

The *Post* article acknowledged that Bean was already famous: "he has become a national institution and a national character." But they defined his market, his customers, as outdoorsmen, as sportsmen, and missed the simple truth that he was not, then, a "national" character . . . fully 90 percent of his business was on the East Coast and in Alaska, a territory where shopping by mail was a necessity. Indeed, Bean's has yet to penetrate the Midwest, the South, or the rural West at anything like their success in the East and scattered suburban cities in California. If the *Post* didn't get the socioeconomic status of the Bean customer quite accurately, they did perceive the essence of the relationship between the Bean customer and the company: ". . . it seems to be an almost universal illusion among his customers . . . that Bean is a personal discovery, to be cherished as a rare and rich curiosity. Bean, as a shrewd businessman, does his best to foster this impression, but it doesn't take much effort. All he really has to do is to be himself."

The snapshot of the company in 1946 is interesting; not more than a hundred employees, except during the Christmas rush, and annual sales of about $1.5 million. When Leon Gorman came aboard in the 1960s, Bean's was doing a mere $3 million. Considering the inflation of prices (a standard item like the eight-inch Maine Hunting Shoe had gone from $8.75 to $22, in those twenty years), Bean's simply did not grow, in fact, it slipped backwards after the *Post* article appeared. Catalog mailings averaged just over 300,000 both spring and fall in the 1940s, climbed up to 400,000 in the '50s, and totaled nearly a million of each catalog in 1967 when Bean died. Return on investment in catalogs was simply not keeping pace with the numbers mailed out. It was one of those oldd synergies between the private man and the publicity — Bean told the *Post* he sold to sportsmen, and the *Post* wrote it, and Bean believed it ever more firmly, and continued, for the next twenty years, to do all of his advertising for new customers in the pages of sportsmen's magazines and the sports pages of a few newspapers.

But even the *Post* could not escape noticing the class of the clientele — George Earle, the governor of Pennsylvania, President and Mrs. Roosevelt, Metropolitan Opera tenor Lauritz Melchior. To them, Bean was a person, and that person was the carefully cultivated image of a Maine storekeeper "with a countryman's personal interest in each of his customers and a sense of the value of a dollar so highly developed that [Bean] is almost as eager to save the customer money as to make money himself."

The classic instance of that sense always was, and the *Post* noted it, the offer to repair Maine Hunting Shoes — "Don't throw away your old leather-top rubbers," Bean warned, using the wartime name when the selling of hunting gear was prohibited. "It is about the same as throwing away a $5.00 bill. Send them to us and we will rebuild them as good as new." That rhetoric, of course, is missing from the current Bean's catalogs, although the offer to repair is still there. Leon Gorman acknowledges that it is expensive goodwill: "I expect we are losing money on it [putting bottoms on the used leather tops], but I'd rather not know how much," he told me.

The one thing the old man did not have in common with his supposed peers, the country storekeepers, was his volubility and sheer noisiness. By the time the magazines discovered him, he was over seventy, partially deaf, and carried on all conversations at a shout. This was, of course, good copy, the kind of local color, uniqueness, that makes a writer's job easy. "In a day when the traditional Yankee passion for trading seems to have been considerably watered down, Bean still takes a frank and lusty pleasure in it," the *Post* gushed.

" 'Gosh, I like it!' [Bean] says explosively, 'My job's not work! The days ain't long enough.' " But even the *Post* had to acknowledge that the sons, particularly Carl, were running the business day to day, and Bean, by 1946, was already taking his months-long vacations to Florida in the winter, and spending most of the summer and fall at one or another of his seven or eight fishing and hunting camps in Maine. The old man recognized the value of the *Post* "write-up" as much as he had understood the value of the prewar piece in *Life*. But this time, he was willing and ready to show his appreciation.

"Over a page and a half [of the *Post* article] consisted of four color pictures," Bean wrote. "To have bought this space would have cost us about $53,000. . . . I tried to show the Saturday Evening Post my appreciation in a substantial manner, but they refused to accept even a gift."

The Curtis family, your basic Eastern Establishment Sports, were already customers of Bean's, and Bean tried to show his appreciation another way:

"Soon after this story came out the head of the publishing company ordered four Hudson's Bay Blankets for his Summer home at Bar Harbor. We tried to make a present of the blankets," he noted, "but they insisted on paying the catalog price."

If Bean didn't understand how journalism worked, he was to benefit in another way from being "discovered" by the *Post*. He would, briefly, become a hero in Maine, where Bean's was just another high-priced catalog before the *Post* piece. Maine newspapers concluded that if he was a hero to the *Post*, they should write columns. A Portland radio station came up the day the *Post* appeared and did a broadcast and Bean was at his avuncular best:

"Mr. Arthur Bartlett, writer for the *Saturday Evening Post*, spent days in my factory getting material for this story, and Mr. David Robbins took over a hundred pictures to illustrate the article," Bean explained. "I was not allowed to change one word of the story, or to select a single photograph."

Bean, who drank Myers's rum, and when he poured you a drink, as they say, you could tell what was in it, was as lavish with praise of the *Post* as it had been of him:

"I have been a reader of the . . . *Post* for a great many years and consider it tops, both in reading matter and advertising. During all these years I have never noticed a single liquor or questionable advertisement."

The radio interviewer asked Bean if he thought "the old-fashioned method of country storekeeping and Yankee trading is going by," and Bean rose like trout to the fly:

"Yes, I am sorry to say it is. The old country store-keeper always tried to see how much he could give for a dollar, whereas many of the modern merchants see how little they can give for a dollar." And on and on he rattled.

The *Post* story would result in a testimonial dinner from his fellow Freeport and Portland businessmen — with the governor of Maine in attendance. For a wonderful thing had happened to L. L. Bean, Inc. For years, it had fed, quite reasonably, off the reputation of the state of Maine for thriftiness, and utility, and canniness. And as the world changed, as Maine itself began to change, as the Sports stopped coming for their month-long stays, as the automobile replaced the train, buckboard, and canoe, it became clear that Bean's, once fashioned in the image of Maine, had itself become the public image from which Maine could profit.

Bean received a curious letter after the big testimonial dinner, from a large gravestone retailer in Portland, Henri Benoit:

> *As a business firm we can well appreciate that the integrity for which the name L. L. Bean stands — all over the world — did not come about by chance. By your efforts and straight forward "down to earth" way of doing business, you have not only brought success to the firm of L. L. Bean, but you have added prestige to the State's business and industry from which all will benefit. . . . Your contribution to Maine is invaluable — it cannot be expressed in mere words, not measured in cold dollars and cents.*

The *Portland Press Herald*, twenty miles south of Freeport, had written a couple of features on Bean in the '30s, no more than they did for other small companies in Cumberland County, and nothing compared to the typical boosterism they bestowed on major Maine industries, the paper companies, the shoe industry, and Portland's own B&M Baked Bean factory. But the *Saturday Evening Post* piece got Bean's picture in the paper (a five-year-old one, but at least a picture) and full coverage of the testimonial dinner. The former chairman of the Maine Development Committee spoke, and no doubt spoke accurately, that Bean had publicized Maine in a way that the committee could never afford. "I can visualize [the *Post* article] to be worth a million dollars to the State," he concluded. Governor Hildreth noted that the catalog, "of which 600,000 copies will have been printed this year [and] which goes to the four corners of the world, strongly suggests to sportsmen to come to Maine, a sportsman's paradise. . . ."

Downtown Freeport, today, is visual proof that Bean's has made a contribution to Maine's economy that is invaluable and is measured in dollars — one boutique after another selling upscale life-style items to the overflow crowds from L. L. Bean, Inc.

The mythology of the *Post* article continued to dominate thinking about L. L. Bean, Inc., into the 1970s. After Bean's grandson, Leon A. Gorman, joined the company in 1960, he realized he would someday be running the company — if he chose to — and when he wanted to find out what L. L. Bean, Inc., was all about, the first thing he did was get a photocopy of the *Post* article and learn it by heart. When, in 1965, the Harvard Business School wrote up a case study on L. L. Bean, Inc., Gorman gave them a copy of the *Post* article, and it was reprinted almost in its entirety as the main body of the case study. Gorman's reliance on the *Post* article is enough to justify our interest in it. Seldom does one see such a clear example of life imitating art, or, business imitating its image in prose.

The old man did nothing in the last twenty-two years of his life to require another major, national story on him, or the company. He would surface from time to time in the national magazines for no particular reason, usually in January or February, after editors had opened their L. L. Bean Christmas presents. The illusion persisted that Bean's was a outdoorsman's supplier — what *Fortune* magazine, in 1955, called "the devoted hardcore of 400,000 U. S. sports enthusiasts [who] eagerly await" his catalog.

Still, by the 1960s, it was becoming clearer that Bean's customer list could hardly be described as hardcore anything, now that it included financier Bernard Baruch, actress Myrna Loy, the Philadelphia (and State Department) Biddles, most of the du Pont family, and the king of Afghanistan, as *Newsweek* breathlessly revealed in 1961. Ignoring his competitors, everyone from Eddie Bauer to the Alaska Sleeping Bag Company, Corcoran's, Herter's, and the rest, *Newsweek* dubbed L.L. "patriarch of the American sporting-goods business, mail-order messiah to the discriminating sportsman." The continuing flickers of national publicity provoked some comment in Maine, but not much. The Maine State Archives, which kept clipping files on prominent citizens, didn't start one on Bean until he died, neither did the special collections department of the University of Maine at Orono. The power of national television news is difficult to assess, but it was indisputably those broadcast obituaries which made Bean famous in his own state.

Country Matters:
the Humor of Maine

FIRST-TIME visitors to Maine expect to find a country-side littered with Bean catalog items. We are disappointed. Maine has turned out to be a sort of extension of the catalog, but not, as it turns out, in the way we anticipated.

One expects the *stuff* in the catalog. Believe me, you can go a long way down the street in Maine before you run into anyone wearing Maine Hunting Shoes or Maine Guide Shirts or sitting on Bean's Best Director's Chair. The basic Maine clothing is the dark green cotton and polyester twill pants and shirts sold in uniform supply stores. This is beginning to change a little, now that Bean's has a discount department in the store, but slowly.

What you get, by and large, is a mirror image of the language in the catalog, everything reversed and upside down and backwards. For the selling language in the catalog, and I mean the old catalog, very little of which remains in the increasingly sanitized material you get today, is best understood as the opposite of the general run of

Maine speech. The original L. L. Bean syntax, "These are the only trout flies you need to carry," is too direct for Maine reticence, and much too abbreviated for Maine loquaciousness — and the native Mainer lives a whole life caught between the poles of saying not enough or saying too much. The catalog language, and the prose of *Hunting-Fishing and Camping* and *My Story,* is compressed, short bursts, explosive; it has neither the flowing rhythm nor the contrived terseness of everyday transactions in Maine.

Maine humor is a consciously practiced art, rehearsed by the natives on each other, as they warm up their abilities for the tourist season. It is done so much that it becomes natural, even in the most trying circumstances. It is not, of course, peculiar to Maine, it is simply the old rural humor, still surviving because it is a way of dealing with the Sports, of coping with the intruders.

The roots are New England–wide, as a famous "Maine" story illustrates. It is the one about the hunters in the Jeep who are driving down the woods road looking for a likely spot to hunt. And they come upon a low spot with a small stream running across the road and they stop to look at it and just then, as must happen, a boy comes out of the woods.

"Sonny," says one of the hunters, "is there a hard bottom there?"

"Yup."

And so the hunters start across the shallow brook and the Jeep sinks to the hubcaps and then to the running board, and as it sinks right to the windshield they scramble back to the high ground and one of them yells at the boy: "You little so and so, you said there was a hard bottom there . . . !"

"So there is," says the lad, "and you are about half way to it."

That exact story, only with an ox cart and set in Concord, Massachusetts, appears in Henry Thoreau's *Walden*. That is what one does to people who forget to ask exactly the right question. It is that withholding of critical information, that deliberate, not particularly attractive, reticence, upon which the bulk of Sport-native transactions is built. The only alternative is utter garrulousness, usually reserved for native-native transactions, rarely visited upon the Sports. Mind you, the laconic style can be put on anyone, at any time.

It is breaking out of that reticence that is difficult, and which makes for the curious inarticulateness of the old L. L. Bean catalog. It is just not normal to volunteer information.

I was walking down the main street of Bucksport with Bud Leavitt on an October afternoon, relishing the quiet. Bucksport in summer is wall-to-wall yachters, antique-hunters, lobster-mavens and people who think they ought to go to Maine on vacation and spend most of the week trying to figure out why they did it. And a man approached us, walking with unusual rapidity and agitation. The conversation went like this:

"What's the matter with you, Ralph?" says Leavitt.

"Oh, Bud, I feel awful. I've got to get up to the drugstore and get an Alka-Seltzer."

"What's wrong, Ralph?"

"Oh, Bud, I was just down to the boatyard. I was trying to get all those summer folk's boats under cover for the winter, and I had this jeezless pile of stuff all over the floor. So, I said, I'll get up in the rafters and nail some cribbin' across them and I'll be able to get some of that mess up off the floor and get some of those boats out of the weather. Well, I was up there, trying to nail these two-by-fours across the rafters and didn't I drop one, and I look down and there's this fellow Bartlett that stores his boat with me. My God, Bud, I've got to get to the drugstore and get that Alka-Seltzer. That two-by-four hit him right square in the head and I looked down and there he was, bleedin' all over the place."

"So what did you say to him?"

"Well," and here he paused for a moment to make sure we were paying close attention, "I looked down at him and I said, 'I thought you was in New York.'"

Note the last question — not "What did you do?" but "What did you say?" It was understood, from the beginning of the monologue, that it would lead up to some expectably terse and laconic final remark. It is not necessary to be a tourist to be the object. The same device was used a few years ago during an election campaign. A Democratic candidate for governor came to Dixmont, near Bangor, to press the flesh and started working Main Street. He ended up in Beazley's grocery store, near closing time, cornering people at the milk cooler and saying "Hello, I'm ————, the Democratic candidate for governor," and so forth. Finally, Beazie pulled the shades and started counting the day's receipts. He had this habit of counting out loud, piling up the change in little piles of a dollar's worth.

So he starts counting the change, muttering as he piles up the quarters, "Twenty-five, fifty, seventy-five, a dollar," and pushing the piles of quarters into a row. And ————, having run out of customers to politic, goes up to the counter to thank Beazley for letting him campaign in the store, and he goes, "Harrumph," and Beazie doesn't look up, he just says, ". . . fifty, seventy-five, a dollar" and pushes another pile of quarters into the row. And the candidate tries saying "Ahem," and he tries saying "Excuse me," and Beazie just keeps going "Twenty-five, fifty . . ."

Finally, the candidate, caught between wanting to get out of there and being polite, just cuts in and says, "Excuse me, Mr. Beazley, but I'm John ———, and I . . ." and Beazley cuts him off right there and says, without looking up:

"I thought you were. Twenty-five, fifty . . ."

Starching someone for being talkative about the obvious is thoroughly Maine, and that can, in some circumstances, mean being thoroughly rude. And sometimes, we deserve it, sometimes not.

I was driving down the west side of Lake Sebago one night in December, during a freezing rain. The road was glazing and I was pedaling very lightly, and as I came around one of the curves there was pickup truck upsidedown on the edge of the road. I think it must have taken me a quarter of a mile to stop, using the low gear to slow down, and then turn around and drive back up to the truck. It was clear off the road, with the cab of the truck out of sight in one of those deep ditches they have to make alongside a road in that wet, cold, climate. So I stopped and I put the flashers on, and walked up to the truck and there was this farmer inside, right upsidedown, holding on to the steering wheel and staring straight ahead. The door was jammed and he didn't have the leverage to push it open. He was bleeding pretty good, the way you will with a facial cut, from a gash on his chin where he'd bounced off the steering wheel.

So I pulled the door open and all I could think of to say was:

"Are you hurt bad?"

And he kept looking straight ahead, holding on to the wheel with his knees on top of what was usually the underside of the dashboard, and he said:

"Hope not."

As I say, the laconic answer is so practiced, so ingrained, the urge to utter it cannot be overcome in the most trying of circumstances.

Well, the volunteer fire department came down from Bridgeton, finally, and got him untangled from the steering wheel and he wasn't hurt bad, but he did take a ride up to Doc Barnes's office, who is the local chiropractor but perfectly able to handle motor emergencies.

I was headed for Sebago, where some friends were going ice fishing, and it turned out they didn't even have the houses out on the ice yet, so I said I would help them. Some of these people I knew all right, and some not at all.

Fish houses are pretty standard, usually built out of full sheets of plywood, so they're generally four feet by four feet by eight feet tall, but not always. And they have wooden runners under them, cut off on a bias on one end to make a ski so you can drag them out on the ice with a snowmobile, or a pickup if there's enough ice.

It always snows before the lake freezes, so you usually have to dig the ice house out of the snow, and usually it's frozen in pretty good, so it means something to help someone get their houses out on the ice; you will get tired chopping them loose and getting the chain around them, and then steadying them while the fellow with the pickup gets them loose and moving and headed for the lake.

I did my share of chopping and prying with a big bar and got down on the frozen mud and got the chain in around the base and feeling fairly confident that it was a job reasonably well done just stood there waiting for the guy with the truck to take up a strain on the chain.

This fellow I didn't know at all was there, driving the pickup, and after a minute he got out of the truck and walked back. I was standing there next to the one I knew best, who ran the general store in Sebago and sold fishing licenses and so forth, his name was Carroll.

"Well," the first fellow says, "Carroll, this friend of yours, he a native?"

"No," says Carroll.

"What with the store, and renting cabins, and selling licenses, you must spend a lot of time talking to out-of-staters, right, Carroll?"

"I do," says Carroll.

"You pretty good at talking to them?"

"I guess so."

"Well, seeing as you have practice at it, and you are good at it," the fellow says, "why don't you tell your friend that he's standing in the effing way and if we start to haul that fish house we'll run it right over him, so you ask him to move."

It is not always so deliberately cruel, but that assumption, that the function of the Sport is to provide what little entertainment there is to be had, runs through a lot of Mainers. My friend Carroll has somehow escaped it. If he didn't want to run a store and go fishing, he wouldn't even have to stay in Maine. He's unusually capable of acting like a normal human being.

It appears that what separates the ones in Maine who don't make a habit out of laconic ragging of the visitors from those who do is that they all have a common human virtue. They are extraordinarily generous. This is remarked upon by their neighbors — you cannot buy them coffee, you cannot go home without a quart of homemade maple syrup or a jar of their mother's corn relish.

The laconic humor is the humor, in the long run, of economic poverty and a certain mean-spiritedness. L. L. Bean almost escaped the mold, as you can see in the occasional moments of generosity to employees. (But not entirely, as seen in that consistent unwillingness to pay more than a nickel over the minimum wage.) Like my friend Carroll, he was able to talk to those out-of-staters, and write the copy for that catalog.

It is almost a truism that whenever a culture has one dominant characteristic, it also shows the exact opposite. Anyone who has lived in a teetotaling countryside knows what that is like. There are practically no social drinkers in places with a strong abolitionist or religious prohibitionism. New Brunswick, up across the border from Maine, seems to have two kinds of drinkers, non, and drunk. The state of Utah is another one with no tradition of social drinking, and the accident statistics to prove it. And, as Maine has the strong tradition of laconic rudeness to the person who doesn't get the question quite right, so, also, it has a number of people of the most outgoing friendliness, and it is L. L. Bean, Inc.'s genius that they have hired so many of them to man the phones at the order desks, and, with somewhat less success, to work in the salesroom. By and large they know everything, every product, and are always extraordinarily sympathetic to your problems, even at 3 A.M., an hour when most human beings cannot do anything right. Such were the staffs of the old sporting camps, who made each summer's vacation a homecoming. These folks are as much a part of Maine as the dry humorists, if, one suspects, somewhat in the minority.

The Clerk's Tale

THE old Bean store was an extension of the old man's personality — functional but muddled, sloppy and somehow efficient. It was not designed. It just grew, like the rest of the business. If it had been consciously planned, if the decision to sell clothing out of the packing boxes was a marketing ploy, not an admission that no one ever took the time to build display shelves, it could best be described as designed to make honest purchasing difficult and shoplifting easy. The mature years, from 1946 to 1966, when the company turned over annual sales of around $3 million, are the ones that customers recall when they talk nostalgically about the old store — L.L. still came to work, and you could find a parking place on the street in Freeport.

A Freeport boy worked his way through college at the old store. His father worked there, his mother too, in Christmas rush season. And his sisters. It was the sardine factory of Freeport. You could work at Bean's or you could move to Portland. Some Maine people, as we noted, have the talent for nonstop storytelling. So let's just listen:

I liked him. You know if you worked for Bean's you didn't work too hard. And you didn't get paid diddly-squat. I never did understand him about that.

He'd get grumpy sometimes, and he'd come down to the salesroom and yell at us and tell us he could replace us all in fifteen minutes. And I guess he could. He was some cute. He'd give you these incremental wage increases, I guess he would hear about what was going to happen, because you'd get the raise and a few days later the minimum wage would go up and you'd be making exactly a nickel over minimum.

He was cheap on the wages, but that wasn't the only way he knew to turn a dollar. I remember, right after the war, he bought all these damn old worn-out leather flight jackets — the fleece-lined ones. I can't remember all the things we used to make out of them. Innersoles for boots. Hat bands to hold trout flies. Stuff like that. Not catalog stuff, just little damn things that laid around on the counters and people would buy them.

Other than wages, and I say, we didn't work too hard most of the time, he was a decent enough person. He gave me a loan for my first house, $4,000, and, I believe the interest rate was around 5.5 percent then, and he gave me the loan for 4 percent and I know I wasn't the only one in town he did that for.

He just didn't care about money. My God, I remember years I worked there they'd do a couple of a million dollars' business and the profit was something like $10,000 or $20,000. Most of the profit walked out the door.

I always worked four to midnight, I was going to college over to Gorham then, so I'd wait till it got quiet and then I'd just sit behind the cash register and do my homework, else we'd play cribbage. There we were, just two of us in the store and maybe a customer wandering around somewhere. Either that or we'd go to sleep. Sometimes the midnight man wouldn't come in and I'd have to stay.

I'd just curl up on the shelf under the cash register. I figured anybody wanted to buy something they'd yell or something.

You know how every damn thing in the store was alway's "Bean's Best." Bean's Best Axe. Bean's Best Snowshoe. Harold, this other clerk, he went to sleep one night right on the checkout counter. So I made up a sign, it said "Bean's Best Clerk." It was just that kind of a place.

It wasn't just petty stuff people took out of there. We had this one stock man working nights, and us two clerks out in front to put up what he brought out. He was, well, I guess he was at least AC-DC. Nice enough old faht but a little peculiar that way. What reminds me of him is these two guys that used to come in almost, oh, twice a week. Real nice guys. They'd see me sitting there trying to study and offer to go across the street to the newspaper store, it was the only thing open besides us, and bring me back some coffee. It got so they were like part of the woodwork. Bring you a lemonade if it was hot, sit around and shoot the breeze, play cribbage with us. Did it for years. Well, one night they were hanging around, one of them playing cards, and some guy came in who wanted shoes. So I couldn't find the shoe that fit him, and I had to go all the way back in the main stock room, which was, you know, sort of across a bridge into another building.

And I get way the hell back in there, it wasn't too brightly lit, and there's one of these guys. I figured he was back there looking for our AC-DC stock man, so I didn't even let on I saw him, and I got the shoes and went back out front.

What it was, it turned out, was these guys were taking stuff out of there by the pickup load. Taking it right out the door. Thomaston graduates, that's what they were. [Thomaston is Maine's one and only state prison.]

Employees weren't much better. I remember this one kid came to work the Christmas season, and he asked if it was true that you could get out the door with something. I said I guessed it did happen. Well, he was a kid I knew from high school, and when we got off work, he said to come over and look at his car. I tell you, I think he had one of every damn thing in that car. It looked like a catalog on wheels. I told him I said I thought it was easy to take stuff, I said I didn't say it was *necessary*.

The funny thing about that was he came up looking for me a couple of weeks later and asked me if I'd help him sneak it back into the store. I guess it got to bothering him. He said he wanted to bring it back but he was scared he'd get caught.

God, it was a jerry-built operation. Believe me, we had more dingies than you could shake a stick at. We had a cleaning lady, I didn't know what to think of her until I got to college. I guess she'd be what you call paranoid. Always figured someone was after her job, so she'd work even harder. Finally they had to let her go, but I tell you, by the end, she was practically running.

This customer, he wanted to use the men's room. Wasn't public exactly, so I took him out back and showed him where it was, and I'm going back out to the salesroom and here comes Gertie, on a dead run as usual, and she busts right in there while he's sitting on the throne and I can hear her saying, just rattling along, "Don't get up, don't get up, I'm just getting a pail of water." Lord, we had more dingies than you could shake a stick at.

That was the damndest store. You could sell anything in there. I mean to say you could sell anything that L.L.

wanted to put in. We had these pewter ashtrays in the sales-room. Kind of cute, had a buck's head and a mallard duck on it, and we sold a million of them at $2.85. Well L.L. came through one day and noticed them for the first time and wasn't he bullshit when he saw them. He didn't want any goddamn souvenirs in his place. I mean that. Just threw them out in the trash. "You don't buy souvenirs at L. L. Bean's store," that's what he was yelling while we were hauling them out. Things are different now. I don't know what he'd think of those L. L. Bean Jeans with people walking around with L. L. Bean on their ass.

You wonder why it took him so long to get those little ashtrays out of there, I think it was that when he got older he had terrible eye problems. Great big man, big flat feet slapping on the floor, and he'd come busting through there on the dead run as usual and he'd just run over some lit-tle kid, couldn't see worth a damn.

He used to come in, start up the front stairs, those big feet pounding and slapping, and we'd all sit real quiet in the salesroom and wait for him to miss that top step. He would just tear through that salesroom going ninety miles an hour, usually yelling at somebody about something.

Ralph Hughes, he managed the salesroom, he was out there one day and it was busy as hell, and here comes L.L., he had a big voice, and, do you know what a firkin is? it's one of those little wooden buckets, we used to sell a lot of those firkins, supposed to put food in them or something, anyhow, here comes L.L. storming through this room full of people and he had that real Maine accent, and he yells: "Ralph, the firkin factory burned down!" I guess he snapped some heads around with that line.

He was always figuring on new stuff. I remember this guy came along and wanted us to bring in archery, so L.L. got a folding chair and set out in the clothing warehouse room, and this fellow put up a target and he was good, shooting arrows, but L.L. wasn't interested in how an expert did it, he asked my dad to try it. Well, Dad shot off about ninety degrees off course and put the arrow right through a carton of chamois shirts. Then I had to try it and I dry-fired the damn thing, the arrow didn't go anywhere and I cut hell out of my hand, fractured the bow, and bled all over the damn floor. We never did put archery in.

I told you we were always having trouble with shoplifters. Once it was a bunch of women from the air base. We knew it was them, but we didn't know what to do about it. So Carl, he was L.L.'s son, Carl had this idea we'd put a one-way mirror in the women's room. I thought that was a hell of an idea and said I'd do the watching but we never did it. That was about Carl's speed. I mean, the old man wasn't the sharpest thing going, couldn't spell worth a damn for one thing, but Carl. Lord.

There were two boys, Carl and Warnie. I guess Warnie's real name was Warren. Warren was okay, he liked his liquor and playing the piano. He'd be in some joint playing the piano all the time. After a while he went to work for L.L.

Carl, he had to have a big office. L.L. would just sit out in the middle, but Carl had the big office. My God, Carl talked so slow it would take him a month to get a sentence out. He had this lump on his head. Like a growth or something. When he got mad, got his blood pressure up, that lump'd turn bright red. You saw him coming with that lump all red, you'd look around quick for something to polish or a place to hide.

I liked the old man. When I was in high school I wanted to go duck hunting, and he knew I didn't have a shotgun. He loaned me his. After a while, I tried to buy it off him, but he said no, he said you take it and keep it and if I want it, I know where it is, I'll come and get it. So I kept it until he died.

That gun was just typical of him. He owned four guns, nothing fancy about any of them. The shotgun I had was twelve-gauge automatic, it was Browning style, but it wasn't even a Browning. Had a great big tubular magazine. I think you could put a dozen shells in it. People that hunted with L.L. they remember him whacking off the whole clip at a duck more than one time. They didn't bother much with the rules down to Merrymeeting in those days.

The other guns, he had an old twenty-gauge Parker. He had a .35 Remington automatic for deer and bear, and some small caliber, maybe a .25 Remington. Automatics, except for the little twenty. All just working guns.

I brought the shotgun back, when he died, and put it right on his desk and left Leon [Gorman] a note. I guess maybe I hoped he'd give it to me, but he didn't.

I took Leon down to Merrymeeting a couple of times. I don't know that he really wanted to be there. I believe he was just studying on duck hunting, like it was something he ought to know about.

[Not to interrupt, but when Leon Gorman had been at Bean's for two years, he told a *Time* reporter that if "I were in another business, I probably wouldn't care much about hunting or fishing, but I'm learning fast."]

Except for the wages thing, L.L. was generous enough. Like the hobo boots. We'd have these Sports that would wear the [size] numbers off the bottom of their hunting boots and figure they needed new bottoms, and we'd save those. And then people would send in the leather tops, you know all you have to send back is the tops, but almost everybody sends the whole damn shoe, and they'd send the tops but not the money, or we'd lose the name, or something, and we'd save those too. Then we'd match them up, and put them together and, well, those were the hobo boots. I guess some hobos did come through town and ask for boots and L.L. would give them a pair. Of course we had boots for the town drunks, the ne'er-do-wells, and the employees. In no particular order.

We didn't make much else besides the boots, and I believe we didn't make anything very clever. You could generally go out and find something nicer, if you looked. But you get people in that store and you could sell anything. Like those damn lounger boots. You can't hardly walk in those things. When I worked there we wouldn't sell a pair of lounger boots a year. We were selling to hunters, and we sold the ten-inch hunting boot, that's what they needed. Now, I know they sell a million of those pull-ons. People go out and start their car in them, I guess.

But you could sell them anything in there. Now L.L. had this Bean's Best Smoking Tobacco. It was a regular brand, we just pasted a different label on it. I believe it might have been old Prince Albert. It doesn't matter. Well, there was always an open can on the counter to try out. Howard Wilson, he was a retired game warden, he'd stand around there and cut up an elastic [known as a rubber band anywhere south and west of Boston] and put it in the open can. You know, you snip up an elastic, it looks exactly like tobacco. Well, those Sports'd light up that stuff and stink up the joint, and they'd stand there and say "This is the best darned tobacco I ever smoked."

L.L. could even sell that little book of his *[Hunting-Fishing and Camping,* or *My Story],* he would get a kick out of sitting there and selling it and having people find out who he was. Then, some days, he'd get one of those clicker-counters and sit at the top of the stairs and count the people and he'd get off on how no one recognized him.

That's the way it was. I don't go over much, anymore.

Bean's Best Friend

GEORGE Soule, who is a fairly good example of what partridge hunting will do for your health, turned seventy in 1983. For thirty years, he was the only other human being who got star billing in L. L. Bean's catalogs. Not only were his Maine Coastal Decoys the ones that L.L. personally used in all his duck hunting, but George's picture appeared in the 1960s and 1970s, his hands cradling the wooden head of one of his cork-bodied black duck decoys.

George is, perhaps, L.L.'s last living friend — not merely an acquaintance, or an employee, or a vendor, but his last companion. He started out as an employee, a Freeport boy, a stock boy in the old man's little company. But it was more than an engaging and open personality that brought the two together.

But friendliness is not the whole story of the relationship between the twenty-year-old stock boy and the old man (L.L. was over fifty when George went to work, somewhere back in the late 1920s). George Soule was one of those characters that turn up anywhere you have a sporting population. He was the man who knew how to do everything: he could tie trout flies, make duck decoys, and find partridge. Not only could he find partridge, something that thousands of men could do, he figured out a way to make it possible for L. L. Bean to *shoot* partridge, and that is a very different thing.

Generally speaking, in a tradition that goes back to the days when the railroads and interurban trolley cars first cut through the New England woods, there have been three ways to hunt partridge, a not very intelligent bird about the size, and shape, of a banty chicken. Casual hunters just cruised the roads, afoot, by horseback, or, as is still done today in the north woods, in pickup trucks. Partridge, like all birds, need daily supplies of grit to add grinding power to their giblets, and roadsides are the easiest and best place to pick up grit. The second method, which was spurred on by the advent of the railroads and trolleys, was a kind of unsportsmanlike but effective combination of roadhunting and shooting over pointing dogs.

In a century when there was little leisure time, most partridge were killed by market gunners, and the birds were sold in Boston and Portland markets from the 1840s (when Francis Parkman, the Harvard historian, used to shoot his own birds, between classes, in the nearby hills of Somerville) to the 1920s, when the birds were finally reserved for the sport hunters. The market gunner was a solitary figure, whose business consisted in knowing where the birds would be, in particular, where they roosted. He operated far outside the usual self-imposed rules of sportsmanship. A bird in a bare tree, outlined against the sky, was worth two in the bush or four on the wing. The era contemporary with the establishment of L. L. Bean's mail-order business saw the introduction of two critical elements in modern bird hunting — the imposition of daily bag limits, which put the emphasis on sport, rather than meat, and the perfection of, as Ernest Hemingway maladroitly, but accurately, called it, "shooting-flying," or wing-shooting.

What George Soule managed to do was perfect the art of communal wing-shooting. Freeport, Maine, back in the 1920s, was the summer home of America's most distinguished author, and artist, on the subject of wing-shooting in general and partridge shooting in particular . . . William Harnden Foster of Concord, Massachusetts, and Freeport, Maine. To say that W. H. Foster was obsessed with partridge would be an understatement. Some of that enthusiasm inevitably rubbed off on his neighbor, the young George Soule. Foster was so obsessed with partridge gunning that he invented the game of skeet.

Persons not familiar with skeet are probably happier than those of us who have suffered with it. Basically, it consists of shooting at small, highly breakable, clay disks with a shotgun. That is like saying that baseball consists of batting, catching, and throwing a leather-covered ball. What Foster invented was a game that duplicated all of the possible shots, all of the possible angles of flight, encountered by a partridge hunter. He used two machines to throw the clay birds, one mounted at ground level, the other fifteen feet up in a tower to imitate the tree-launched partridge. The gunner moved from the base of one tower to the other, along a half-circle, stopping at seven stations so that all of the possible angles were encountered. The last station is number eight, directly between the towers, where the gunner gets the rarer, but not at all unlikely, shot at clay pigeons imitating birds flying directly at him. The first skeet field in the world was constructed in Freeport, within earshot of George Soule.

If William Harndon Foster was the archetypical Sport, with time, money, good dogs, and fine shotguns, a man whose partridge gunning was ceremonial, cerebral, and social, George Soule developed a style that would endear him to L. L. Bean. George invented the one-beater partridge drive. Shooting driven birds is, usually, the perquisite of landed gentry, orthodontists, and international financiers. It requires, ordinarily, vast acreages, dozens of hired hands, and a large company of gentlepersons with shotguns. An army of beaters scatters in a thin line across the meadows and heaths, and slowly and deliberately pushes the birds (European partridges and pheasants) toward the assembled line of gunners. This requires a special geography, as well as money, and there is no place in Maine where you can line up a hundred beaters and twenty gunners and hope that anything practical will come of it. Driven game is for hedgerow and heath country, not alder swamps and old orchards overgrown with tangles of catbrier and swamp cedar.

George Soule happened upon a style of hunting that was the perfect solution for Maine, and for L. L. Bean, his employer. Soule discovered that partridge were in the same places and at the same times of day, something known to every serious upland game bird hunter, and took it a step further than William Harnden Foster ever did, or ever wanted to do. Soule learned that the birds also flew out of their covers by the same routes, day after day, and thus he invented the one-man partridge drive. Gunners (it takes more than one, as most birds have more than one preferred exit) would be stationed in ambush, and George Soule would head down the middle of the cover with his dog. Partridge covers are usually little bits of countryside, and Soule learned hundreds of them in the Freeport area. It is an impressive sight, or would be, if the terrain, the thick growth, did not make it almost invisible — George Soule and one of his American water spaniels, pushing through the brambles, and friends and acquaintances carefully posted at the exits from the covers. George Soule got his shots, at flushing birds, and the assembled company got theirs, at birds pouring out of the hardwoods, birds flying forty miles an hour, birds very much like high-tower station-eight skeet shots.

"So," Soule explained, "L.L. would come out in the middle of the day and look at me, and he'd say, "Looks like a good pa'tridge day, George, and don't bother to punch out [on the time clock]' and I wouldn't. We did that a lot."

But George Soule was more than a hunting guide for the old man, George was handy. His first manufacturing job at L. L. Bean's was running the fly-tying department. Like a lot of the manufacturing at Bean's, the company got it into it out of sloppy management, rather than by choice. "The trouble with Bean's," he explained, "was that for a long time they weren't set up to estimate anything. That's how we got into fly-tying. At first just to tie a few to fill in the orders we didn't have in stock. Then, we got into it. One time, I had sixteen girls tying for us."

Bean's got out of the fly-tying business right after World War II. "You know what did it?" Soule asked. "What happened was at the end of the war, in all those military hospitals, they taught fly-tying for therapy. All those guys came home and set up businesses. That was the end of fly-tying as far as doing it in the company."

The decoy business was a direct result of George Soule's becoming L.L.'s guide and hunting companion. They had had a miserable day shooting, a stiff wind consistently toppling their decoys, and L.L. asked Soule if he couldn't make a better decoy. It was, Soule thinks, around 1934.

"So I went down to Portland. I had cork on my mind, I thought it would be the stuff to use. Found a couple of old ice trucks in a junkyard, and pulled the cork insulation out of them. It seemed to work fine."

From 1935 to 1975, cork worked just fine for George Soule. By the 1950s he was turning out over ten thousand "working" decoys a year, and as that business failed to grow much, started adding a line of decorative decoys. By the time he retired in 1975, the production of purely decorative decoys was a third of the business. Before quitting, George Soule had made almost a third of a million decoys, and sold almost all of them through the Bean catalog.

L.L.'s shooting style was hardly scientific. Although he owned a little custom-built twenty-gauge, his standard hunting implement was a twelve-gauge Remington automatic that had, before and even after it was legal, an extension on the magazine. The standard Remington held one shell in the chamber and five in the magazine, and Bean's gun had a five-shot extension, giving him eleven live rounds. "He could handle that great clumsy thing," George Soule recalled, "although it sometimes confused him. I remember one time he opened up on a duck and kept hammering at it [as it flew away]. He was absolutely convinced that he killed that bird on the seventh or eighth shot. Well, it wasn't anything but a speck by then. It had been some earlier he shot it, it just took that long to go down. But I do recall, in fact, he once shot a grouse with the fifth shot."

L.L., George Soule thinks, "was an awful nice man. And he was an interesting guy to talk to. He didn't just talk. He listened. That was how he learned things, really. As far as talking went, it was a two-way street as far as he was concerned." Soule acknowledges that Bean wasn't the most generous paymaster, but points out that neither was anyone else back during the Depression. "The main thing, I think," he will add, "is that L.L. had some pretty pinching times himself."

The Maine Coastal Decoys, and the smaller hand-painted little decorative decoys, are still fabricated in Freeport, on the machinery that George Soule adapted to decoy making. Heads and bodies are fashioned sixteen at a time on a shaping lathe that was originally designed for furniture manufacturing. The unfinished decorative decoys are put out to a half-dozen local housewives and mothers of young children who paint them at home and turn them back to the Decoy Shop. About half the ten thousand decorative decoys made each year are sold through the catalog, the rest marketed through gift shops. The hunting, corkbodied decoys are almost all sold through Bean's, although the Decoy Shop tries to keep some semblance of independence by selling a few through sporting goods stores. As with so many products in the catalog, however, a retailer has great difficulty matching prices with L. L. Bean. As usual, Bean is buying at a lower wholesale price (around $11 in 1983 for a standard coastal decoy) and marking them up less (to $18) than would be normal retailing practice.

There are a number of reasons for the slow growth in working decoys, compared to decorative, some of the same forces that are shifting the mix in the Bean catalog. Duck hunting, nationally, becomes more and more the province of clubs and leased rights, and new hunters find themselves with a choice between a hunting organization that has already built the blinds and bought the decoys, and fending for themselves on diminishing, and overcrowded, public lands. Meanwhile, as the number of hunters goes up and the number of ducks, in most parts of the country, and most particularly in the East, the heart of the L. L. Bean market, goes down dramatically, seasonal limits make decoys something of a joke. By the 1983–1984 duck season, most eastern Sports were limited to one black duck a day, and the black duck is the premier target from Maine to North Carolina. It is difficult to justify a boat and a spread of decoys for one duck.

Even if you have them, it may not be worth going out, which means that nothing gets worn out, broken, or lost. Eastern duck hunting becomes, for the average man, a few hours spent jump-shooting (walking-up ducks) on coastal marshes or a day's jump-shooting from a canoe, early in the season. The number of living rooms, game rooms, and dens in need of a decorative decoy is a larger, more stable, market. It has gotten so bad, that by the 1983 season, George Soule was wondering if he would bother to go duck hunting. He lives on the bay, his boats are on the water, and he can look out his living room window at the island where the decoys toppled in the wind, the island where L. L. Bean had his hunting camp, and even that close to it, wonder if it is worthwhile, anymore. "One black duck. It seems like a waste to get set up for one black duck." Bean's old camp is long gone, the victim of vandalism. Freeport, today, is just another suburb of Portland, and along with too many people come a few hard cases. Along with too many people come too few ducks. The sporting world changes, and George Soule is slowly letting go of it, spending more time hunting quail in the warmer southland, less time worrying about decoys, and ducks.

George Soule, looking back on a life, sees the place of his invention in the scheme of things: "I know they will keep the decoys in the catalog," he says. "I have heard that they are worried about losing their sporting image."

L.L. Lets Go . . .
a Little

LEON A. Gorman may have been L. L. Bean's favorite grandchild, but it is likelier that he was simply the child of L.L.'s favorite offspring, and only daughter, Barbara. When Leon Gorman's father died, L.L. encouraged him to come into the business, something Gorman was probably planning to do eventually, as he had taken a job as buyer for Filene's department store in Boston, after four years as a naval officer. Gorman joined the company in 1960, as the clothing buyer, following in his father's place. "It was the only empty desk," he has remarked, "and so I sat down and did the job that went with the desk."

The year was 1960, and the salary was $80 a week. The company was rolling along under L.L.'s part-time guidance and management by Carl Bean, Gorman's uncle. It turned over two and half million dollars in sales that year, with a net profit, after taxes, of $42,000. Included in the expenses, besides Gorman's $4,160 salary, were the salaries for L.L. himself and Carl Bean, whose combined income was less than $80,000 in straight salary. It was a remarkably sleepy company, whose employees averaged sixty-two years of age, and whose average salary, excluding the two elder Beans from the calculation, was about $5,000. Except for the executives, the highest-paid workers were the moccasin-stitchers, some of whom were taking home as much as $7,000 in piecework wages.

The difference between Leon Gorman and everyone else at Bean's became quickly evident. As a member of the family, and one of the five buyers (a buyer each for clothing, shoes, fishing tackle/sporting goods, hardware, plus one for items for the factory store that were not included in the catalog), Gorman was automatically a member of what passed for an executive council for L. L. Bean, Inc. He was the only executive at Bean's who had ever worked anywhere else, and he could, evidently, hardly believe his eyes.

The mailing list for the L. L. Bean catalog in 1960 totaled 430,000 names. Each got four mailings a year, the hundred-page spring and fall catalogs, and two thirty-page small books, the summer and Christmas catalogs. The entire mailing list was hand-typed, in duplicate, twice each year, a pair of labels for spring and summer, another pair of labels, reflecting any additions or deletions, for the fall and Christmas books, 1,172,000 typewritten labels. Young Leon's first idea was buying, or renting, an Addressograph machine. In the days before computer-generated and automatically printed addresses, the Addressograph Company was the latest thing in automation. Pieces of aluminum, looking like squared-off GI dog tags, were embossed with a name and address, and then fed automatically, one piece at a time into a printing machine that inked labels, or whole envelopes, with considerable speed. Gorman brought the idea up at the board meeting, and it was dismissed out of hand. They had always typed the labels, hadn't they, and they were making money, weren't they? Old customers of Bean's will recall that not only did they get a hand-typed label, but they got their catalog completely enclosed in a sealed brown envelope. It looked like real mail, not junk mail (and there was hardly any junk mail in 1960).

Even worse than Leon Gorman's idea of purchasing an Addressograph machine was the suggestion that Bean's hire a Chicago mail-order service company to fulfill the obligations of the list — that would have meant a Chicago postmark under the old Postal Service rules, and L.L. had much too much sense to imagine mailing from anywhere but Maine — not even the brash young grandson stood up for *that* idea. In addition, L.L. was employing twenty-five women full time who did nothing but type labels and stuff the envelopes. He might have paid the minimum wage plus a nickel, but he had no intention of laying anyone off. Bean saw the label-typing pool as a source of trained, loyal help during the Christmas rush. Gorman never got his Addressograph machine — by the time he was in charge, the mailing list was converted to computer storage and printing.

He did win one argument the first year. The mailing list, which was the source of $1.8 million worth of business in 1960, existed in only one copy — on paper — located right in the old firetrap of a wooden building that was then both the retail store and the factory. Gorman convinced the management that they might want to have a duplicate list, and they might want to keep it in a fireproof place — like a bank vault. That idea, which did nothing to upset the system, was accepted.

For the next four years, Gorman worked quietly, within the system. L.L. was clearly failing in health, and the business was being run by Carl Bean, with Gorman as his principal assistant. Gorman, by attrition, acquired more jobs at Bean's. He continued as clothing buyer, and took charge of supervising the retail store (and did nothing to change it), supervising the mailing list and catalog production and mailing (and very definitely did not buy an Addressograph machine), and supervising purchasing for all the company's products (that is, the technical details of ordering and paying for goods; the departmental buyers continued to pick the products and order the quantity anticipated to be necessary to fulfill future sales). He was also Carl's personal assistant. It was a cordial relationship, on the surface, although anyone asking Leon Gorman what he thought of Carl is likely to be greeted with a shrug of the shoulders, a roll of the eyes, and a look, in an unguarded moment, of distaste. But Carl was sixty when Leon Gorman came on board, and Leon Gorman planned on waiting. He would have to wait until 1967, when L.L. died, and Carl was retired, to go much farther with his plans.

His only triumph, in the years of no power, was to overcome the great Interstate Highway Disaster. In 1955, the retail outlet in Freeport did almost $500,000 in business, which accounted, as near as anyone can recall, for a third of Bean's total sales — the largest market share for the retail store in the history of the company. And in 1955, the first New England fruits of Dwight Eisenhower's defense program — the interstate highway system — bypassed Freeport. The Maine Turnpike (in New England, it is not uncommon to combine federal highway systems with toll roads) ran from the border to Portland, and in 1955, they continued it north toward Augusta, the state capital, and built a toll-free spur, from north of Portland to the coastal town of Brunswick, east of Freeport. That effectively bypassed L. L. Bean's, and the next year, sales in the retail store dropped to $411,000, and by 1958, store sales hit their modern low, a mere $395,000. They grew slowly for the next few years, as the price of goods also rose, but store sales were down around 20 percent of total volume and not growing. Gorman's single administrative success, prior to taking over the company, was fairly simple. He talked L.L. and Uncle Carl into putting in a parking lot across the side street from the store, so that the harried visitor had a chance at a place to park, without giving up and heading back for the interstate and his destination. The year the parking lot went in, 1963, store sales bounced from 1962's $456,000 up to $527,000. The next year, when the word got around, they jumped again, to $609,000. Gorman was managing the store, and the sales were increasing by 12 to 15 percent a year, while the company as a whole was growing by 1 or 2 percent. Without the increase in store sales, Bean's would have been losing ground in absolute terms, and was, in fact, losing ground in constant dollars, discounting inflation.

Leon Gorman had discovered something important: Bean's was a money machine, if you could keep it running smoothly. If he could get customers coming in the door of his own department, the retail store, he could sell goods, make money, and have some sense of purpose. Making money, growing, that was what businesses were supposed to do. Besides the retail store, Gorman's major responsibilities were in the catalog and mailing-list departments, and he started to learn the major lesson of his life at L. L. Bean: There was an absolute and positive relationship between how many catalogs you mailed and how many dollars came back in the door.

Leon Gorman, like many a man, was under the impression that the way to get customers was to advertise. And he kicked up the advertising budget in a few short years to $50,000. He spent most of it in *Sports Afield, Outdoor Life,*

Field & Stream, and *True*. (*True*, in case you never saw a copy, was "The Magazine for Men," a sort of cross between *Outdoor Life* and *Soldier of Fortune*, running heavily to war reminiscences and dead fish.) He also, inexplicably, bought advertising space in the *New Yorker*. But, in the 1960s, Bean's had no way of knowing which advertisements were working — which ones were pulling new inquiries and new customers. The whole typewritten mailing list system militated against any analysis. It came as rather a shock to Gorman, several years later, to find out that of the five magazines he had chosen, the *New Yorker* was a much better advertising buy than any of the outdoor magazines. He has, in fact, never quite been happy with that fact. He does not, an executive once remarked, like to be reminded of it, at all.

But wherever the responses to the advertisements were coming from, they were not generating a great deal of business. The average growth of the company, excluding the retail store, was still lagging around 2 percent annually.

Fundamentally, Gorman could not separate the customer-generating advertisement from the inquiry-generating advertisement, and, even more problematic, he did not really know who the hardcore L. L. Bean customer was. He was trapped, not in his own ignorance, but in the disinformation system created by L. L. Bean — twenty-five superannuated ladies clicking away at typewriters had the keys to the kingdom locked up in the rolls of gummed address labels, and there was no way to decipher the code until the computer arrived. Not only was the system designed to keep one from learning much about the customer, Leon Gorman had read that article in the *Saturday Evening Post*, and believed it. But young Gorman was already making a distinction between his view of the customers and his grandfather's. "He doesn't care about money," Gorman told a reporter in 1962. "Grandpa likes the people who buy from us because they're hunters or campers, not because they're customers."

If Gorman was stuck in the mud, so was every other supervisor in the company. Interviews conducted by students at the Harvard Business School in 1965 make that clear. (What prompted them to bother with a $3 million company is not recorded, but I suggest that the Harbard/Bean connection is as solid as the Harvard/Unitarian connection, and the Unitarian-Universalists and the Bean customer list are virtually identical.)

The purchasers for clothing (Gorman) and shoes, tackle, hardware, and the factory store accounted to no one. There was no policy to decide whether an item, particularly shoes and other leather goods, should be manufactured by Bean's or bought on the outside. There was no inventory control system — none. The buyers were expected to keep track of what amounts of their goods were sold annually, and keep their own inventory by visual inspection of the warehouse — mere guesstimates of quantities on hand were made. Buyers made their own forecasts and purchased goods on their own authority.

If inventory was difficult for the buyers to estimate, it was a horror show for the people who picked items out of inventory and packaged customers' orders. Mr. Arthur Griffen, the fishing tackle manager, mentioned to the Harvard investigators that he thought it would be a good idea to have catalog numbers for the items. Bean's was carrying over a thousand items in the catalog (about eleven thousand items, if you count all the various sizes and colors), and there weren't any numbers attached in 1965. You ordered the red shirt on page 17, that's what you did. And every stock picker had to know the catalog by heart, and the locations of the stock in the stock room by heart. It was a mess at holiday season.

The accounting system, except for gross expenses and income, simply did not exist. There was no breakdown at all, it was as if the thousand items were one. There was only a fuzzy separation of catalog sales profits from retail store profits (and the cost of mailing different objects was totally unknown, and unaccounted for). Storage costs and cartage costs to get the goods into the warehouse were not separated by item — just lumped together as if the $1,000 worth of axes was as expensive to lug around as the $1,000 worth of men's shirts.

If accounting didn't exist, manufacturing was a palpable mess. It was scattered on three floors, in two separate buildings, with machines interspersed between stock rooms and little elbows of the retail store that jutted back into the manufacturing areas. There were, for all the thousands of shoes and belts and Bean bags being built in 1965, only thirty-six employees directly involved in production, with an average age of sixty, just under the company's overall average of sixty-two. While Freeport (and all of Maine) was filled with out-of-work manufacturing employees in 1965, few of them wanted to go to work at Bean's. The other shoe companies, including three closed in the greater Portland area in 1964, had always paid piecework, and if you hustled, you could make a living. When the production manager suggested an incentive program, Carl Bean nixed it, quoting L.L.'s famous dictum, "I'd rather see an employee do a quality job than hurry and anyway, I eat three good meals a day and couldn't eat a fourth." Whether the employees were eating three good meals a day, is, of course, another question, and one that never really troubled the old man. Not that he was uninterested in the employees' well-being, he just never included money in his concept of wellness. If the government said a minimum wage was a good idea, it was fine with L.L., he added a nickel on top, and gave out an end of the year bonus to regular employees. (A bonus that continues, although Leon Gorman once referred to it as a "tax gimmick on top of an incentive plan.")

When the head of manufacturing suggested moving the leather-stitching machines from one corner of the building to put them next to the leather-cutting machines (and eliminating a trip across two buildings and through a dumbwaiter for the goods), L.L. said no. He said that some of those people had been sitting in the same spot for thirty and forty years, and would resent being moved. This, of course, described the old man perfectly. He had been sitting on the same spot for fifty years, and he didn't want to move, either.

The Harvard folks ended with an interview with Gorman, the evident heir-apparent, as Carl was sixty-four and L.L., at three years before his death, was hardly in charge. Gorman had faith in the company, that it had not exploited pure mail-order as far as it could. They should stay in the same business, "concentrating on hunting, fishing and camping," he told the interviewers, "upgrading and improving an essentially static line." The era of 50-percent women's goods was far from his imagination in 1964. Gorman had ideas about how to do that, how to stay in the outdoors field and grow. Primary goals included a form of cost accounting that would lead to understanding the profitability of individual items in the catalog, and some kind of accurate control over inventory. Gorman thought it would be nice also to have an accounting system that differentiated between the expense of manufacturing and the expense related to sales. He dreamed of some logical organization, perhaps bringing in an outside consulting firm to help him plan. He was even considering — and that was heresy — bringing in "professional outside help as a part of management" and, even, as a member of the corporate board.

The Harvard summary captures Gorman's problems almost poignantly, as you look back from 1984's $230 million company to 1964's $3 million company — "Even though he had recently been thwarted in making major changes, Mr. Gorman felt he should consider and list these and other changes that might have to made in the future, arrange them by priority, and plan how they could best be phased into the company's operations."

A generation of Harvard Business School students have mused over those problems, those options, since L. L. Bean became a "case" in 1965. Whatever they have thought, whatever options they have considered, one suspects they could not have done more to change L. L. Bean's finances than quiet, patient Leon Gorman, and his happy band of fifty-odd executives. But between that day in 1964 when he talked, nay, dreamed, of a better L. L. Bean, Inc., and the success story of the past ten years, there would be a difficult period, from 1967, the year the old man died, to the mid-'70s, when he finally got a management team on board. The company would grow in sales, but not without difficulty, much of it of Gorman's making. For he would cause the company to grow faster than he could manage it.

Leon Gorman
Takes Command

WHEN L. L. Bean died in the spring of 1967, Leon Gorman had been president of the company for three years. Uncle Carl had retired at sixty-four, in 1964. But Gorman had done nothing, while L.L. was alive, to change a single system or move a single person, inside the company. The ambitious heir would be able to have his way from 1967 onwards — automated mailing lists and all. And he would run the company single-handedly for the next eight years, working sixty and seventy hours a week, until he found himself riding a tiger — the company would grow much faster than his ability to manage it, faster than any single, all-governing, chief executive could control. But, as he brought in one new manager after another in the 1970s, these first eight years would be critical training, those eight years would create a hardness and a toughness and a sense of power in Leon Gorman. He might add managers, take advice from specialists, but, to this day, he continues to run the company out of his own office, with his own motives, relying as much on his own intuition as any marketing scheme, product analysis, or financial plan brought onto his desk.

They were fascinating years, as Leon Gorman made the company grow, but managed to make it grow without fundamental changes. It was the era of "more of the same." There was no real change in the product mix in the catalog, or the method of getting new customers — display advertising in national magazines and high-circulation newspapers. But, simply by working the old system harder, Gorman would increase sales from $3.8 million in 1966 to $20.4 million in 1974. By keeping an eye on the store, including cutting employee theft and improving inventory control, Gorman pushed net profit from $85,000 (2.2 percent of sales) in 1966 to $1.3 million (6.5 percent of sales) in 1974. The old system of assessing inventory by visual inspection ended in 1969, when a local accounting firm was hired to keep track of it. Curiously, although the inventory counting task was hired out, the internal operation of the company was not altered — goods were still ordered, received, warehoused, and shipped by the old methods — but Gorman now had an outside agency keeping track of the goods. Employee thefts, long a problem, began to drop off quickly as shortages not accounted for by sales figures were brought to the attention of warehouse and salesroom supervisors.

Superficially, there were great changes — in 1969, two years after he took over, Leon A. Gorman put carpeting on the stairs that lead from Main Street to the second-floor salesroom of L. L. Bean's factory store. This event remains a subject of nervous laughter at L. L. Bean, for it was the outward and visible sign of the new era. The carpet story is always the same, although attributed, in various Bean-supplied versions, as either a phone call, a letter, or a conversation on the streets of Freeport, and the substance is always the same. The crusty old-time customer says: "Place ain't been the same since they put carpet on the stairs."

Although that is the company line, the truth is the place hasn't been the same since they put the carpet on the stairs, put carpet on every salesroom floor, put fake barn boards on the walls, put souvenir-priced articles in the store, and put away the open free sample can of Bean's Best Pipe Tobacco and put up the No Smoking signs, among other radical changes. The constant reference to carpeting the stairs (a few years later they also widened the stairs) is a kind of "aw, shucks" form of public relations, an attempt, usually successful, to deflect interest from the real, significant changes, such as — and it absolutely altered the character of the store forever — introducing the use of credit cards.

Not everything Gorman did in those first years worked perfectly. He continued, and increased the budget for, advertisements in the major sporting life magazines; that these advertisements were not particularly cost-efficient would be something he would not learn until the mid-1970s. But the amazing growth in sales (other mail-order firms were having trouble averaging 10 percent growth over the same seven-year period) was simply the result of increased numbers of customers, and that could be easily traced to the overall advertising budget. As total sales went from just under $4 million to slightly over $20 million, a five-fold increase, Gorman increased the magazine advertising budget from $50,000 to $200,000, a fourfold increase. Additional customers were gathered, for the first time, by soliciting names and addresses in the factory salesroom, a place that had traditionally been run as if it were in another world from the rest of the company.

More importantly, Gorman began to tinker with the

advertising system, something L.L. and Carl had never bothered to do. For the first time, magazine advertisements carried different street addresses on Main St. (All irrelevant, as L. L. Bean, Inc., had its own Zip code). Most of the advertisements (he had expanded to sixty-four magazines and newspapers by 1974) also offered a specific item for sale. This small innovation, at first intended merely to increase the catalog mailing list, turned out to be L. L. Bean's first information on the varying power of advertisements in different magazines. If they had no way to be sure which magazine was drawing requests for catalogs, they could at least see which magazines were producing the most orders for merchandise. Thus, Gorman was able to keep track of purchases made from each advertisement and estimate the real cost of advertising in a specific magazine or newspaper. Responses with orders for the advertised item were so satisfactory from some magazines that there was, as Gorman described it, a "negative cost" for doing business.

While still in the hand-tabulation era, Gorman was also able to, for the first time, keep track of the relationship between first inquiries and first purchases, and determine that, year in and year out, 25 percent of the people who wrote in for a catalog would buy something within the fiscal year. (Bean's fiscal year reflects its historic dependence on the fall/Christmas shopping season, and ends on February 28, by which time not only can the Christmas business be calculated, but most of the returns and refunds have been made.)

As sophisticated as the system was, compared to the old days, it was telling Gorman almost nothing about the customer — it was only telling him a little bit about the advertising media he had chosen. All sensible mail-order houses calculate a "cost-per-inquiry" figure, a simple division of the number of inquiries generated by an advertisement into the advertising expense. What Gorman began to dream about was something entirely different, and much more difficult to store and understand — the dollars of sales generated by each inquiry, keyed to the advertisement that brought the inquiry. He wanted some kind of system, and it would have to be computerized, that would code customers' names with the advertisement that had generated their inquiries, and keep track of them for their buying life. But that would have to wait until he had answered the fundamental question — how big should L. L. Bean, Inc., become?

As it was, he was having considerable trouble keeping the company up to speed, making sure it could swallow the 20 percent annual growth in sales that his expanded advertising campaign was generating. As sales grew, so did the number and frequency of out-of-stock items. The system for forecasting sales of a specific item, simply looking at the previous year's results and multiplying by a factor of 10 or 15 percent, was breaking down, because the company exceeded its predicted growth every single year, and continued to do so until 1983–1984. As the volume of letters from customers, most of them wondering where the promised goods were, increased, Gorman began to hire specialists to handle the mail — five service managers to begin with, each with a specific area: clothing, footwear, fishing and hunting gear, camping, and miscellaneous.

Even that system began to break down in the early '70s, and Gorman hired his first outside consultants, a mass-mailing firm, to sort out the program for responding to customer complaints and questions. The old system of responding to complaints with individual letters was dropped, temporarily, in favor of preprinted forms, as the consultant convinced Gorman that speed was more important than personality. The mailing consultant also introduced one of the first real speed-up management techniques at L. L. Bean. The customer-service desks, typical office desks with file drawers, were removed and replaced with bench-type desks. As the incoming mail was sorted and shipped to the specialists, a colored tag was stapled to the top of the letter, and the color was changed every week. Supervisors of the customer-service specialists could just walk down the aisle and visually tell which letters had not been answered within one week. Speed is still the goal at Bean's, but in the ten years since the mail consultant started the form-letter response, Bean's has tried every conceivable method of answering letters: handwritten notes on the back of the customer's own letter, automatically typed responses (that always included either a minor spelling error, or a struck-over letter, to give the illusion of a unique, personal response) and various form letters. The current system involves phone calls when possible (they're cheaper than individually typed letters), computer-generated printouts for out-of-stock items (either offering a refund, or giving a promised date of delivery), and the ersatz personal letter with the deliberate, small, error in it.

It is part of the integrity of Gorman, and L. L. Bean, that the first outside marketing consultant went to work on customer service, but the next contributions from the world of direct-mail consulting would really start the catalog, the retail store, and the image of the company down a slippery slope toward today, away from the individualism, the idiosyncratic nature, of the old man, the old company.

Leon Gorman took over Bean's in an era perfectly suited, perfectly timed, to his goal of growth. The thing that really made the company grow, or, that made growth possible, was not of his doing. It was a federal government device, the six-digit Zip code, that changed the very universe that L. L. Bean operated in. It took the direct-mail industry about ten years, from 1964, when Zip codes became commonly used across the country, to the mid-1970s, to perfect the general theory of Zip-code mailing. Massive data bases have been accumulated that combine three elements:

1. Street directory names and addresses, culled from voting and tax lists of smaller towns and suburbs, or from the typical printed street directories available for larger U.S. cities.

2. Census data, either federal or private, that indicates the average income of persons residing in Zip-code areas, which can be small enough to separate out the upscale and trendy parts of a tired city — that can separate the Back Bay and Beacon Hill area of Boston from the working-class and poor black sections of the city.

3. The Zip code itself, as an extraordinarily cheap and rapid way of sorting a list, ever so much faster than alphabetical searching, ever so much more accurate than street name sorting (there are over fifty Washington Streets in Boston and environs, and not all of them are filled with likely customers for penny loafers and chamois cloth shirts).

What Zip-code-based mailing would do for the mail-order industry is make it possible to send catalogs, each personally addressed, to a list of people who would very likely have desirable incomes and house styles (you can separate out the parts of a city with mostly apartment dwellers from the parts with backyards, for example, and sell house-plants by mail in the first area, and trees and shrubs in the second area).

It is not a system that can entirely replace advertising-generated inquiries, but it is a powerful system for occasional mass mailings. Several years ago, for example, a

Bean executive proudly noted that over 70 percent of the households in a wealthy suburb of Boston and another, equally wealthy, suburb of San Francisco, were receiving L. L. Bean catalogs. This was in the days just before the perfection of Zip-code mailing. Today, anyone who has the money can put a catalog in 100 percent of the households in a Weston, Massachusetts, a Grosse Pointe, Michigan, or a Tiburon, California. Whether you can sell anything is another question, but the customer list, and the potential customer list, once the most closely guarded of business secrets, is now available to anyone with the money to rent one.

While Gorman was trying every possible program to maintain the close link between Bean's and the customer, he was not interested in imposing his own personality on the process. Changes in the catalog copy indicated the passing of the founder: the past tense replaced the present and the chamois shirt became the "shirt Mr. Bean always *wore* on his hunting and fishing trips."

Gorman is, and always has been, a reticent person. He regularly assigns one of his vice-presidents the task of making charitable donations and accepting awards. He is reflective, intuitive, and keenly interested in the psychological makeup of his employees. When it became clear that Bean's could not survive its rapid growth without some kind of full-scale data-processing systems in the building, Gorman hired a data-processing expert to plan the system, and started to worry about the employees' ability to shift over from the shouted instructions and the handwritten orders to keypunching and printouts. And simultaneously, he hired a Portland industrial psychologist to give aptitude and personality tests to prospective supervisory employees, and to conduct interviews with potential senior-level managers and department heads. The emphasis was on matching characteristics and jobs, and, more particularly, on matching an applicant's psychological type with the existing personalities in the Bean organization. What Gorman wanted was a friction-free management team. He, after all, had operated for his first four years under the thumb of Uncle Carl, and for the first seven years under the eye of a somewhat erratic, often absent, but always dictatorial L.L.

While Gorman continued to run a virtual one-man show, he hired a comptroller to start to put some hard numbers on what had been, for sixty years, a series of guesses — how many employees should be hired, how much extra warehouse space should be built or leased, how much cash would be needed to pay for goods delivered. He was running a $30 million company by 1975, as the economy rebounded sharply from the OPEC shortages of the winter of 1973–74, and he was running it with a pencil. Every morning, a handwritten report arrived from the mail room, showing how many orders had been received the previous day and how many orders on the comparable day in the previous year. He also got reports from order entry (where a customer's order was translated, by hand, onto picking and packing orders), from shipping, from accounting, and from customer service that showed how many orders they had handled, and how many orders were pending — in short, what day's mail was being handled, and how far behind they were. Gorman entered these morning reports on a single large piece of paper — the whole flow of a company, of fifteen million different customer orders, all in his own handwriting. If that gave Gorman the feeling that he knew what was going on, he once remarked to a Harvard interviewer, it was not clear whether anyone else knew what was going on. For example, since the company's basic work force, perhaps 75 percent of all employees, were involved in entering orders, and picking, packing, and shipping orders, it should have been easy to predict Tuesday's workload from Monday's mail reports. While department heads could have used the mail report for that, Gorman "doubted that they used the information" for any purpose.

Cost accounting was almost nonexistent as the company reached the $30 million level. Cash flow remained close to historical standards — an average order, discounted for inflation, remained about the same, the customers bought most of the same items, and counting the mail was still the single most useful tool for guessing the week's cash income and product outflow. Departments — manufacturing or shipping or receiving — simply did not have budgets, everything was done as it always had been done, by a group of managers that averaged thirty years of employment with Bean's. They did it the old way, and Gorman let them continue to, while he kept an eye on the pennies. The only cost-accounting device in the company was a simple monthly statement that showed the *variance* of department expenditures over the comparable month the year before. The amount of useful information in the variance reports was questionable, as a sample provided to the Harvard Business School indicates. The September 1974 Expense Variances report notes that account number 7091, Advertising, direct mail space, paid out $44,885 more in 1974 than in 1973 with the cryptic explanation: "Sept. 74 paid seven invoices from Ad agency — Last year paid none during month of September." There is not even a hint as to where the company was on its scheduled payments for the year. The variance in account 8240, Factory-manufacturing supplies, was less money, but more detail. The variance was $238 according to the controller, but the items, $114 for trash removal, $52 for small tools, and $63 for "four stools purchased from Lewiston Shoe Machinery Company," added up to $229.

The one thing Leon Gorman did know was that the business was outgrowing the downtown location — manufacturing, warehousing and shipping were still going on in the main buildings in Freeport, and in leased space near town. He made the decision, in 1970, to build a new corporate headquarters, warehouse/shipping facility, and manufacturing space a half-mile down the road. It was a difficult decision, psychologically, because it meant more than separating the retail store from the manufacturing and shipping departments, it meant committing the company to continued growth. There was no point in building a new structure for a $30 million company; he would have to guess the size of the company three years down the road, when the new building would be designed and completed, and then three to five years beyond that, since there was no point in starting another building as soon as the first one was finished. Giving up the leased manufacturing and warehouse space meant, he said at the time, giving up forever the idea of "pulling our horns in," if things didn't work out. Forever, it turns out, came in 1983, when Leon Gorman canceled plans to build several hundred thousand square feet of storage buildings, the year that he stopped growing the company.

The one thing that was clear to him was that for Bean to continue to grow at 20 percent a year, it would not, could not, rely on some general upsurge in recreational spending by the people he thought were its customers — hunters and fishermen. Government statistics indicated that while disposable personal income was rising by about 7 percent a year during Gorman's first ten years as the president of L. L. Bean, the increase in the number of hunting and fishing licenses sold each year was lagging far behind, rising only 3 percent a year. More ominously, for a recreational company, there was clearly no leisuretime boom in the making. The year that L.L. died, Americans spent about 1.1 percent of their disposable income on *all* forms of recreation — six years later, they were spending a negligibly larger 1.2 percent on recreation. There was no way to grow the business by letting it tag along with the national income. There had to be an aggressive effort to cut out a larger piece of the economy than the stagnant recreational budget.

The other choice was almost unthinkable — the company would have to grow by reaching the nonsporting consumer. That was not one of the possibilities that Leon Gorman considered in 1974.

The decision to build the new headquarters, to abandon the comfortable, safe way, put another serious burden on Leon Gorman. He was responsible for almost four hundred employees, and the family stockholders of L. L. Bean, Inc. L.L. had gotten away with being a one-man show by living until he was ninety-two, and by keeping the company the same size for the last forty years of his life. If the company was committed to growing, and something happened to Leon Gorman — everyone was in trouble. He promoted an employee to right-hand man in 1973, hoping to train him up to be able to run the company in the case of his own illness, an accident, or his death, and it didn't work. The right-hand man was let go, and Leon Gorman went outside the company, and outside the state of Maine, to look for a principle assistant. Naturally, he wrote the Harvard Business School.

He asked the alumni placement office to help him find a "Merchandise Manager," someone to "be in charge of all buying and buyers for our catalog and retail store, as well as product development, testing, and evaluation . . .

[and] our retail store operations," and "long range marketing planning." In short, a manager of everything that matters in a merchandising enterprise.

Gorman explained, "He would report directly to me and should have sufficient capability in other areas of business to act as my understudy, being capable of running the business in the event of my death or disability. I am 39," Gorman continued, "so there is no guarantee he will succeed me — only that he should have the ability to do so if something unforeseen happens to me."

Gorman listed a number of other desirable qualifications for his right-hand man, and then described the really essential ingredients:

> *He must have a strong, personal, and proven interest in some of our outdoor sports such as fly fishing, upland game or duck hunting, family camping, backpacking, canoe camping, or cross country skiing. Plus an interest in country living.*

It is fair to say that what Leon Gorman wanted was, in fact, someone to play the merchandising role that L. L. Bean had performed so naturally for so many years — Gorman's own interests in the outdoors were fairly specialized. He liked fishing, but only went hunting out of a sort of social necessity and self-image enhancement. He particularly liked the more solitary sports, riding his tenspeed bicycle in the summer, cross-country skiing in the winter. The number-one assistant had to carry the heavier freight of hunting, and high-country camping, he would have to be the consummate woodsman, the nimrod.

There was, however, one major difference between this ideal candidate and L. L. Bean. Gorman did not want a character. The new man, he explained to the alumni office, must "have a 'low-key' personality." If there was a genuine L.L. clone out there, Leon Gorman didn't want to meet him.

The successful candidate was Bill End, a twenty-six-year-old with a Master of Business Administration degree from Harvard and three years' experience — as a product marketing manager for the Gillette Company in Boston. Recently divorced, and a passionate hunter, fisherman, and cold-weather camper, the chance to move to L. L. Bean, and live in the woods, was a heaven-sent opportunity to the young man from Boston. He, with Leon Gorman's approval, was to bring L. L. Bean, Inc. into the modern era of direct-mail marketing, for better or for worse.

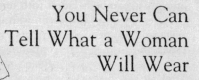

You Never Can
Tell What a Woman
Will Wear

WHEN Bill End arrived in Freeport in 1975, he didn't know any more about direct-mail marketing than L. L. Bean did sixty years earlier. But he knew how to find out about it, and he knew where to go to hire people who already had mastered those skills. Within five years, End and Gorman had hired sixty-six college graduates (fifteen with MBAs) for a management team that built the business from $30 million to $120 million between 1975 and 1980, and would grow it up to $225 million by 1983. The new crowd descended on Freeport like Forty-Niners on the mother lode. There was pure gold in the L. L. Bean image, and they were the men to glean it. Perhaps Forty-Niners is not the best analogy, the new managers at Bean's were really technicians — mining engineers and assayers of the ore. The old man was more of a prospector, trying one product after another, following his instincts up cripple creeks, trying out products like the all-rubber union suit, occasionally tripping over a real winner, like the chamois cloth shirt. The new breed at Bean were like the mining managers who could take low-grade ore finds, or ancient streambeds laden with microscopic flecks of gold, particles too small to be seen with the naked eye, and make millions from them. Modern gold discoveries aren't mother lodes, they're just dirt, contaminated with gold.

Leon Gorman wanted Bean's to grow. That is the point, after all, of businesses, which are perpetual children, and when they stop growing, in the eyes of their owners, they are dead. Gorman and End set a goal — they wanted to move from $30 million to $60 million by 1981 — a five-year plan that would begin with the 1976 fiscal year. That kind of controlled growth matched their physical plant — the new building on L. L. Lane, just off Route 1 on the outskirts of Freeport, was intended to handle that much inventory. They missed their target by a mere $112 million — actual gross sales in 1981 (ending February 28, 1982) were $172.3 million. Business had more than quintupled. From the day Gorman and End started cranking up the system, it has been catch-up time in Freeport — the employee workforce added six hundred hourly employees, another four hundred part-time employees, just to keep the product flowing out the doors. Of more than ninety salaried executives added in the same time, thirty were data-processing and materials-handling specialists.

Bill End began a process in 1976 that was, perhaps, inevitable. He started, with the help of an outside consultant, asking questions about the nature of the Bean customers: who were they, where did they live, how did they perceive the company? This is routine stuff in merchandising, but if you pause and think about it, it is also exactly the opposite of the method that created Bean's in the first place. The old man began with a specific product and went looking for customers who needed it. He thought, in the beginning, that his customers would be woodsmen like himself, and as he became older, more interested in creature comforts, he had attracted a few hundred thousand loyal customers who wanted soft shirts and comfortable shoes and warm blankes. He sold things he liked and things used by like-minded people. "L.L. *knew* who his customers were," one of the young executives at Bean's remarked one day, "they were Sports." Bill End didn't know who the customers were, and that process of finding out, something the company does every year, in one sophisticated form after another, would provide much of the information that has irrevocably changed the shape, the very nature, of the company.

The first thing he found out was that about one-quarter of the company's customer's were women in 1975, a larger fraction than you might expect from a company dedicated to serving Sports. But the old demographic pattern, the one that L.L. sensed, continued to hold true — the Bean customer was, like the Sport, an educated, professional person. Nearly 40 percent of Bean's customers have done graduate work, 26 percent have a bachelor's degree — only 16 percent of the American population has gone as far as the B.A. In family income, the Bean customer is a salesman's dream — 70 percent of them earned more than $27,000 a year (in 1981), and nearly 40 percent of the customers were making over $40,000 that year — when only 25 percent of American households managed to make more than $25,000. And the old geographic ties were there — the same Eastern Megalopolis that sent Sports to Maine and their children to summer camp provided Bean's with half of its customers — the New England and Mid-Atlantic States, plus the Baltimore-Washington nexus. Another 15 percent came from the industrial and mercantile cities along the Great Lakes, from Cleveland to Milwaukee. Bean's geographic and economic customer profile is indistinguishable from that of any Ivy League college alumni association. And Preppies, after all, are nothing but the children of Sports.

But these people were hardly hardcore outdoor jocks. They put their Bean purchases on for leisure wear more than any other purpose. Wearing it "around the house" was slightly more common than wearing it outdoors, and nearly as many women wore their Bean gear to work as wore it outdoors. This comes as no surprise to this reporter. I have seen more Maine Hunting Shoes on the patrons of the Lincoln, Massachusetts, Sanitary Land Fill than I ever have in the woods of Maine. As a matter of fact, if fifteen years of casual observation makes a fact, Bill End is the only person I know who actually wears L. L. Bean Maine Hunting Shoes while hunting partridge. And driving to work each day, passing through the streetcar suburb of Belmont, Massachusetts, you can see the young architects with their rolls of drawings and their Maine Hunting Shoes, waiting for the electric trolley that runs into Harvard Square. The only person, other than Bill End, whom I ever saw dressed head to toe, hat to shoes, in Bean gear was a computer programmer on his way to work in the Square.

Gorman and End had decided to concentrate on mail-order sales, before they started scientifically studying their customers. The choices had been three — to increase their manufacturing base, making more of their own product line; to increase their retail store sales, perhaps by opening a branch store near the Maine–New Hampshire border, or to work on the mail-order business. The reasons for picking mail order were varied, but the predominate one was simple — if sales are directly related to the number of potential customers reached by a catalog, theoretically, you can manage your growth, keep it at the proper pace, by managing the number of catalogs you mail.

There were two basic sources for new names — the advertising budget was increased from $250,000 in 1975 to over a million dollars by 1980. But no money was poured down a rat hole. End, working with the new computer-based customer-listing system, was able to keep track of each new customer added by advertising, and watch the customer's buying performance over the years. This was the major breakthrough in advertisement placement, and from the late 1970s on, Bean's advertisements would appear more and more in general circulation magazines and newspaper sections aimed at the young, the affluent, the educated. As a rule of thumb, you can find an L. L. Bean advertisement in any magazine or newspaper that has an Italian vermouth ad — more recently, any place that you see a Perrier advertisement. The expanded advertising program was gathering in over 800,000 names a year by 1980.

The second source for names was a common practice in the industry, but new to L. L. Bean — renting mailing lists. End bought the rights to 400,000 names in 1975, working with rental lists that seemed appropriate places to find Bean customers — the obvious ones were companies like Eddie Bauer, the mountaineering-oriented company, but End had realized that the basic outline of Bean's own customer list had less to do with the outdoors than with age, income, and status. He rented lists from F.A.O. Schwartz, the home of expensive toys, and Yield House, purveyor of expensive bric-a-brac, home furnishings, and dry goods. By 1980, Bean's was mailing to almost five million new names a year gathered from other companies' mailing lists.

The broader advertising campaign, and the move into mailing lists leased from companies that featured home products and women's clothing, had a predictable effect. The percentage of women on Bean's customer list doubled by 1980 to 50 percent, and the catalog began to reflect it. On the company's own terms, the number of pages devoted to women's apparel jumped from eleven to sixteen, and women's shoes added an eighth page. What that does not indicate is how many items once offered only in men's sizes, particularly boots, shirts, and parkas, were being offered in men's and women's sizes by the 1980s. The net increase in women's clothing, including the increase in what had once been men's products that were being offered in women's cut and size, was on the order of 100 percent, exactly matching the increase in the percentage of women customers.

The six extra pages (the fall and spring catalogs averaged 126 pages through the 1975–1980 era) given over to women's wear were extracted from sporting equipment, as were the two extra pages of what Bean's likes to call Home-Camp Furnishings — that is, sporty-looking housewares for the sporty wife to dust, wash, or use. While the main money-makers in the Bean catalog continue to be all of the versions of the Maine Hunting Shoe, followed by all the varieties of the chamois cloth shirt, individual items of women's clothing have become the single-style leaders. The move to women's clothing remains controversial within the company.

The primary advocate of women's wear was the vice-president in charge of product, Charlie Kessler, one of Bean's many Harvard MBAs. Kessler, with a background in department-store merchandising, saw the Bean customer as just another person with money to spend, and fought for the gentrification of the catalog from the day he arrived. Kessler qualifies, in some ways, as a hardcore outdoor jock, in Bill End's terms, but he is really more of a Sport — the kind of person who loves to go duck hunting but can't bear to remove the inedible insides from ducks. Kessler has fretted, over the years, at the difficulty of getting Bean's up to speed on women's wear — Bill End was one brake shoe on that express, and so are the infamous "categories." The categories are to L. L. Bean, Inc., what the kosher laws are to the Orthodox. Everything must fit into that categorical rubric of what is acceptable, else it cannot be included in the catalog. Sporting goods is a broad category that accommodates everything from skis to trout flies and tents. It is easy to add a sporting good item — Leon Gorman is a bicyclist, and as soon as he was in charge, Bean's added bicycle gear. The three clothing categories, and there are only three in the world of L. L. Bean, are: footwear, outerwear, underwear. When Bean decided to get aboard the jogging craze, footwear was able to absorb running shoes without any trouble. But running suits? They really weren't outerwear in Beam terms, which meant stuff you wore in the woods or shirts you could wear to the office. After a year's hesitation, they added jogging suits, which, for accounting purposes, are regarded as "underwear."

Bean's women's outerwear had been standard for years: sweaters, parkas, wrap-around skirts, dressy oxford cloth shirts for the office, and pants cut to women's sizes and shapes (a sort of baggy cut, predating Gloria Vanderbilt's denims for the well-fed matron). Kessler recognized the opportunities in women's wear, if it could be made more fashionable. He could knock the socks off the department stores with Bean's 35 to 50 percent markup over wholesale, and Bean's wholesale purchase price, as they buy in volume greater than even large chain department stores, is typically 75 percent of normal wholesale. In 1981, he got the corduroy shirt dress into the catalog, and it was so popular it was almost disastrous. "A practical dress for Fall wear," the catalog described it, "Made of soft, narrow wale

81% cotton, 19% polyester corduroy." Priced at $29 that year, it was back-ordered to the tune of more than five thousand dresses during the pre-Christmas weeks. The relationship between a dressy dress and outerwear is dubious, but Kessler had no illusions about the whole program in women's wear. "Everything new in women's wear is a twelve-to-eighteen month fight," he once told me. His biggest triumph over the system was the introduction of the extremely dressy wool blazer for women. (Bean has resisted following down the path of the Orvis Company, or its major competitor, Land's End, and has not offered any sport coats for men. When they are ready, there is a historical example, of which we will speak in a minute or two.) "I said the blazer was a piece of outerwear," Kessler said with a look of fierce determination, "and I won that one." But, when asked what possible connection there might be between dressy street wear and the category of outerwear, Kessler threw his hands up in mock horror: "Well," he laughed, "you just can't predict what a woman will wear outdoors. I mean, look at what some of them wear to go fishing!"

Kessler, as product manager, is responsible for more than putting things into the catalog — he takes things out. With the advent of modern computers, Bean's can calculate the exact profitability of every single item in the catalog, month by month, penny by penny. There have been major casualties caused by strict profit and loss accounting — one of the first to go in the modern regime was the Maine Warden's Jacket. For those of you who do not remember the postwar Bean's catalog, the Maine Warden's Jacket was "designed by a game warden," it was green, it had a zillion pockets, and it was made out of wool. Those of us who have been in Maine, and been Sports, didn't order very many Maine Warden Jackets, but a lot of us thought about it, and would, when the fall catalog arrived, once again read the description and imagine how we would feel, walking to class or going to work with a warm, long, green, many-pocketed jacket. Leon Gorman liked having the Warden's Jacket in the catalog — his father and L.L. had collaborated in defining and ordering the originals, and it was something of an institution in the men's outerwear line.

"Yes, Leon wanted to keep the jacket," Kessler once said, "and it took me three years to get it out of the catalog. The customer," he continued, in words that become more prophetic about the future of L. L. Bean, Inc. than I imagined on hearing them the first time, "*The customer was telling us he wasn't interested.*" And that raises the fundamental question of where you go with the Bean product line — there are a lot of things in the catalog that don't pay their way — all of the fishing tackle, most of the tents and sleeping bags, Bean's Best Axe, among them. Another casualty of the profitability judgment was the only sports jacket Bean's ever sold. (The current offering, a Norfolk jacket, is, technically, a hunting coat — the function of the two bands of extra material that descend from the shoulders to the jacket side pockets is to provide support for the pockets when they are filled with shotgun shells.) The old Bean's sport jacket was a black and white houndstooth check, with flapless side pockets, and no padding in the shoulders. It was cheap to make and cheap to sell. Unfortunately, unlike chino pants or chamois cloth shirts, it looked cheap, not functional.

Bill End played the conservative on the intramural squabbles over the direction of the company, partly out of loyalty to the old days, partly out of a deeply understood knowledge of the relationship between the image of L. L. Bean and the continuing success of the company: "You can't knock things out [of the catalog] just because they aren't paying their way," he told me. Some of those unprofitable items are the real difference between the Bean catalog and their competitors' glossier offerings: "I just believe that we wouldn't sell the casual clothing if we didn't have duck decoys in the book," he said. The seductiveness of women's casual clothing is simple: as with the shirt dress, Bean's can market a common item at less mark-up than a typical retail store, and play to that market they have developed: the under-thirty-five, $30,000-plus-income woman of today.

"The easiest thing to do," End said, "is get into women's clothing and make a zillion dollars. But I think that would be a short-term profit bonanza at the expense of the company. If you want a guaranteed disaster, continue the shift towards women's apparel."

As Bean's sends more and more catalogs to its regular customers (I, and three million others, get a minimum of *nine* catalogs a year, sometimes twelve) the shift to women's clothing and housewares is particularly marked in the extra catalogs — after the 136-page spring and fall books, there are additional books, approximately half-size spring, fall, Christmas, and winter catalogs, with seventy-two pages. There are even some quarter-size books of forty-eight pages, and in these, which actually make up 70 percent of the pages of goods a customer sees in a year, the dominance of women's products is startling. There are duck decoys, but they are there for show. A typical half-size catalog, the 1983 "Early Autumn," showed thirteen pages of women's wear, and four pages of camp/home gear — nearly half the book directed to the women's market. If you think of it in terms of how many times Bean's reaches your house, seven out of nine, or ten out of twelve times, you are getting a catalog heavily oriented to women's wear, gifts, and home furnishings.

That was the sort of path, that journey toward a loss of

identity, that the original Abercrombie & Fitch followed to its demise. Once known as the store that outfitted arctic expeditions and big game hunters, A&F found out they could market anything to their loyal customers, people who could afford African safaris and trout fishing in Chile. Their wonderful San Francisco branch store, hard by Gump's oriental arts store and the San Francisco Brooks Brothers branch, was a truly great fishing tackle outlet. There were oak drawers of trout flies, each arranged by the major rivers of the West. You could walk in and buy exactly the right local fly for the McKenzie River in Oregon, or the Madison River in Montana, and not only that, but the clerks knew the seasonal appearance of the flies through the year, and would sell you the greenbodied wet McKenzie special in May, and the orange-bodied dry fly imago of the McKenzie special in June. But to buy that fly, you had to beat your way through a thicket of table lamps, a morass of tweedy jackets and embossed leather wastepaper baskets. The New York store was even worse. They had a full-scale gun department on the sixth floor, with first-class gunsmithing done right on the premises, but that was on top of five floors of furniture, $5,000 leather toys, and elephant-foot wastepaper baskets. Abercrombie & Fitch failed, only to be revived, in name only, a few years later. It is now an upscale mail-order and suburban shopping mall business, owned by Oshman's, a Texas-based sporting goods company.

It would be possible to exaggerate Bill End's role as the conservative-jock in the corporate structure, but he is clearly the hardest-core outdoorsman anywhere near the top. Leon Gorman is equally conservative, if less dedicated to hunting. One of the things Bean's has done in the past ten years is pay more attention to the product lines of their competitors, only fair enough, as the core of the

Bean clothing line, the chamois cloth shirt, is found in every single competitor's catalog. Bean buyers noticed, as early as 1978, that their major competitors all had a Norwegian-knit sweater in *their* catalogs. It was nubbly, a mix of white and blue yarns, and Leon Gorman didn't like it. He didn't like it for six years. He said he didn't like the color. Well, finally, either he got used to the color or the buyer finally brought in a sample in a better color, and now, along with Bauer and Land's End and Orvis, etc., you can get what Bean's calls its Blue Rock sweater. But if Gorman is conservative, holding on to the Maine Warden's Jacket for a few years, fighting off the Norwegian sweater for a few years, he is not about to impose his personal taste on the entire product line, or fight forever. "We have to go where the customer wants us to go," he said once, talking about the shift to women's clothing. But he and Bill End created the woman customer, they made her more than 50 percent of their market. It becomes a question of who is leading and who is following, down that path to becoming a women's sportswear book.

Bill End is not a stubborn person. But he is one of the few executives to get products into the catalog because they belong there — because they work, rather than because they sell. He is a high-country trophy hunter, capable of camping out overnight at twelve thousand feet in the Brooks Range of Alaska, sleeping next to a mountain goat carcass, keeping the grizzly bears away from it, and he can get up in the morning, skin out his trophy, butcher the flesh, make up a two-hundred-pound backpack of hide, horns, and meat, and walk it back to camp. He does not really look like a mountain man — he's average height, and does not have Leon Gorman's natural slimness. The long jaunts to Alaska have to be preceded with months of dieting and jogging. He is responsible for one of the few really new items in the holy category of men's under-wear — the line of tufted-pile polypropylene-yarn cold-weather gear. It works in Alaska, which is not something that can be said for women's three-button blazers, or jog-ging suits.

Both Gorman and End, from different perspectives, understand that it is not just that duck decoys sell wom-en's clothing, but that the sporting goods sell everything in the catalog. They have, for instance, kept a line of fishing tackle in the catalog that would have disappeared as quickly as the Maine Warden's Coat if cost accounting was the is-sue. In the retail store, fishing tackle earns a princely $400 a square foot per year — a good department store will av-erage $250 a square foot. But fishing tackle is nothing compared to the women's clothing area (unlike the cata-log, the store is semiorganized) which averages $1,600 a square foot. That does not mean fishing tackle is out — the job of the average buyer at Bean's is to find, pur-chase, and sell goods at an annual growth rate of 20 per-cent, at a minimum. The job of the fishing tackle buyer, a very pleasant young man, is to not lose money for the company. He is the only person in the buyers department with so genial a task.

If Bill End is convinced to keep hard sporting goods in the catalog for image reasons, Leon Gorman has a slightly different perspective. Gorman is always thinking about the *customer*, as his grandfather taught him to do, but Gor-man is obliged to think about several million more cus-tomers than L.L. ever dreamed of having, half of them women. "We have seen the emergence of women to their proper role in society," Gorman told me once, and then, philosophically, noted that Bean's could not "refuse to of-fer what our customers want." And they want shirt dresses and oxford shirts in women's styles, that's what they want.

After men's outerwear, women's apparel is Bean's second largest category for sales — nearly 25 percent of the gross sales in any year since 1981. Women's wear is well ahead of men's footwear, well ahead, indeed, of the store's best item, the Maine Hunting Shoe. Gorman can be defensive about the feminization of the catalog: "It was L.L. who put the ladies' department in the retail store so that they would have something to do while their husbands were shopping," he argued. Then, reflectively, he returned to thinking about the impact of the customer on his company: "We are not entirely in control of our destiny," he said.

The one thing we do know is that if Destiny has a face, it's wearing lipstick. From 1978 to 1984, 70 percent of Bean's new customers were women.

Preppies,
Disposable Income,
and the New Leisure Class

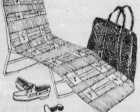

I T is a truism of the direct-mail marketing world that a customer who shops by mail from one company is a better-than-random prospect for another company — thus the trading of mailing lists, or the purchase of brokered mailing lists, is a major industry. L. L. Bean was one of the last companies to exchange lists — the old man was jealous of "his" customers, and Leon Gorman moved very cautiously for the first ten years he headed the company.

The simple explanation for the usefulness of brokered and traded lists is that mail-order purchasing is a habit, and he who buys seeds from W. Atlee Burpee will buy red handkerchiefs from L. L. Bean, or trout flies from Orvis. But list-renters and list-swappers have discovered that the mere habit of buying by mail is not sufficient to justify the cost of mailing to anyone on a mail-order house's customer list.

In the orginal specialty market — gardening products — list trading is endemic, because there is little purpose in hustling All-American vegetable seeds to apartment dwellers, or people who just hate gardening in general and zucchini in particular. A single purchase from the Park Seed Company should ensure you of at least six seed catalogs the following winter, and if you are lucky in the list-swapping lottery, a dozen. And it is a lottery. When mail-order houses buy a list, even a list that seems perfectly adapted to their market, as when one seed company buys another's list — they typically sample it. The computer (everything is on a computer these days, there's no reason to hold *that* against L. L. Bean, Inc.) randomly chooses 5 or 10 percent of the addresses, and the first year the company mails only to that list. The returns (usually identified by using a special box number, or a code on the return mailing label) are then weighed against the cost of printing and mailing.

For years, even after Leon Gorman took over and began to trade lists, Bean, Inc. thought it was a specialty house — outfitting the Sport, his wife, their "camp kitchen," and their summer-camp-bound children. The old man spent millions, over the years, advertising for customers in *Fin, Fur and Feather, Outdoor Life, Field & Stream,* and *Sports Afield.* When Leon Gorman and his right-hand man, vice-president Bill End, started tuning up the Bean's mailing list, they tried customer lists of other sporting goods companies and found them less satisfactory, on a sales-per-mailing return, than the new names added directly to their own mailing list through advertisements. There was something fundamentally different between the prospective Bean customer and the existing customer of a competitor.

When Bean's finally agreed to swap lists with some of the higher-priced outdoor specialists — Orvis, for example — the sales-per-mailing improved, but not dramatically. To this date, the company has found nothing tha works better than finding the customer through advertisements in print media. For one thing, Bean is assured that the inquirer actually wanted to look at the catalog. The best new customer, their marketing research indicates, is a person who already buys something, anything, by mail, but has *chosen* to add Bean's to the pile of catalogs on the kitchen table.

Who buys from Bean's is a complex question, best taken up after looking at who buys by mail in the first place — by identifying that larger constituency before singling out the Mainiacs, Sports, Preppies, and Trendies who send their cash to Freeport.

Mail order is a nearly $30 billion industry in the United States — and the old giants, Sears and Montgomery-Ward, account for over $2 billion themselves, megabucks more than Bean's $230 million in 1983. Once the general store for the rural world, most direct-mail today is directed at the upper-middle-class, and that includes the seed catalogs, now heavily dominated by houseplants, exotic flowers, and expensive hybrid shrubs and trees.

The world of mail order is split into general merchandisers and specialties. The Sears/Montgomery-Ward group, and the local department stores with catalog sales (they're all doing it), and the oil and travel card catalogs make up the generalists — they have about $10 billion of the nation's business. The specialists, from books to sporting goods, grab the other $20 billion. If you throw out the largest mail-order specialty, which is various forms of medical and life insurance, and photo finishing, which is really selling a service, not a product, and stick to the merchandisers of goods, then sporting goods, at around $1 billion, is the sixth largest category. The leader is home furnishings, housewares, and gifts, at $3 billion, followed by books ($1.5 billion), manufactured "collectibles" (over

$1 billion), and cosmetics, at nearly $1 billion. Then comes sporting goods, but Bean's, of course, is not locked into sporting goods — a typical 1980s catalog is 20 percent home furnishings, and about half of the eighty pages of footwear and clothing is for leisuretime, or business, wear, as opposed to hardcore outdoors. Bean's probably belongs, although it is never counted, in the generalist camp. That it might be, someday, just another all-purpose catalog, is a thought that continues to haunt the company.

The mail-order customer is one of the least studied animals in the world, and marketing to that customer is largely a matter of guesswork and refined experience. Some companies are superb collectors of information on their own customers, although they are seldom able to translate that into action. They know what works, but after the fact. Executives at Bean's still tend to look at the results of mail-list sampling with more amazement than understanding. But once they have tripped across a good list, a good advertising placement, or a good Zip-code sorting system, they know very well how to manipulate the information and keep the customer list growing.

The few reputable academic studies, done in the 1960s and '70s, indicated that the mail-order buyer had one important quality — the mail buyer had above-average income. Early studies tended to lump two kinds of stay-at-homes together — what the *Journal of Retailing* calls "in-home shoppers." There is a distinct difference between the mail-order in-home shopper and the in-home shopper who purchases from door-to-door salespersons. Women who buy cosmetics from sales representatives while at home are distinctly less well off than women who choose not to. Other than income, studies found no psychological traits that separated the in-home cosmetics buyer from the department and drugstore shoppers. Early studies of mail-order shoppers turned up the sociological distinctions — the head of the household tended to have a more prestigious, as well as a more lucrative, job than the heads of non-catalog-shopping households.

A massive study carried out in Michigan in 1970 gathered enough respondents to sort them by the type of mail-order purchasing they did: large general-purpose catalog and department store catalog purchasers; people who bought such things as fruit or processed food in the "item-a-month" programs; the pure novelty catalog buyers, specialty catalogs, credit card membership catalogs, and people who bought by mail from newspaper or magazine advertisements.

In 1970, when the study was done, L. L. Bean fitted neatly into the specialty catalog category. Today's Bean catalog is edging into the general, department store, market, since you can buy a wide variety of street clothing and household utensils, as well as sporting gear. This has been a tendency of all the successful specialty catalogs. Orvis, presumably a fishing tackle company, now gathers much more than half its $10 million of mail-order business from sales of china, glassware, and tweed jackets. Brookstone, before it was purchased by Quaker Oats, sold tools and materials for woodworking, metalworking, automotive, and electrical hobbyists. Today it is at least 50 percent gourmet cooking and housewares.

The Michigan study of catalog shoppers looked for a set of attitudes in the buyers and nonbuyers, and they are of interest to anyone trying to understand the Bean shopper. The study looked for different degrees of six personality traits:

1. trust in people
2. cosmopolitanism
3. attitude toward credit as a means of purchasing
4. feelings about impulse buying

    5. adventurousness
    6. conservatism.

In addition, the study looked at several sociological aspects of the buyers, including:

    1. occupation of the head of the household
    2. educational level of the head of the household
    3. total family income
    4. social class.

(Non-sociologists and other ordinary, sensible people, might wonder if "social class" wasn't just the sum of occupation, education, and income, but be patient. It's going to turn out that it might as well be, after we look at the study.)

There were a number of ways to predict whether a person would or wouldn't be a catalog shopper, based on these personality and social traits, and the best one of all was social class — the higher the status of the family, the more likely they were to buy by mail. Not surprisingly, since occupation and social class are almost inseparable in the United States, the next best predictor, even better than total income, was something defined as "cosmopolitanism," loosely, that set of attitudes and experiences which keep you from being a local yokel. (Cosmopolitanism should not be confused with mere adventurousness — it is not the willingness to take risks, but rather an attitude that sees new experiences as a normal part of life, rather than potentially risky or unpleasant.)

Useful in guessing whether a person would buy by mail, but not as useful as the big three — high social class, prestigious occupation and cosmopolitanism — were total income, educational level, and conservatism. (Conservatism in this sense is not politics, but is the opposite of mere adventurousness — it is maintaining habits in the face of disorientation — in Conrad Aiken's memorable phrase, "I tie my tie the way my father did / On a tilting planet . . .")

That is the complex of attributes that make up the whole class of mail-order purchasers — but if the same questions are asked just of the people who order only from specialty-houses, all the variables stay the same, except that conservatism becomes one of the most important attributes of these specialty purchasers — compared to people who buy from all-purpose, novelty, or fruit-of-the-month clubs.

Now, let us consider the Sport, L.L.'s best customer. The Sport had enough time, and disposable income, to take the train to Maine and stay in the camp. The real Sport also could afford membership in the great trout clubs and Atlantic salmon clubs from Maine through the Canadian Maritimes. As membership in these clubs is, and was, more exclusive than membership in a New York or Boston men's club, the Sport had at least upper-middle-class status, and if he was not in banking, or the stock market, he was almost certain to be a lawyer or a doctor. There is, by and large, no stuffier a crew in creation than a collection of Sports in a salmon camp.

And let us consider the mini-Sport, the Preppie, the upscale urban dweller, those people who are the best customers of L. L. Bean, Inc., those customers that Leon Gorman found, by the millions, after the old man died. Assume you wanted to reach, by advertising, a class of people with high-status jobs, advanced education, considerable income, and high social class. On the East Coast, there is one premium medium for reaching them, and that is the Arts and Leisure section of the Sunday *New York Times.* And that is one place where L. L. Bean's, Inc., advertises, week in and week out. The next logical place is the *Times* Sunday magazine, and L. L. Bean, Inc., is there. And the *New Yorker*, right in there amidst the perfume and the cognac, and the long stories about childhood in India,

Bean's is there. The old man didn't know about these things. He kept after the outdoor magazines, and the *sports* pages of newspapers, including the *Times*. In Boston, Bean's advertises in the *Globe*, but in the Sunday magazine section, right in there among the Jordan Marsh and Filene's fashion advertisements, the gourmet recipes with four-color illustrations, all the trendiness that characterizes that newspaper section.

There are some other nonsurprising places to advertise for new Bean's customers — given the social set, you can guess them as well as, say, a Bean's executive. You, too, would advertise in the *Wall Street Journal* and *Barrons Weekly*. Bean's continues to advertise in the outdoor magazines, but more from a sense of duty, a sense of tradition, than because the returns are worth the investment. The big-city slick magazines have been tried and found wanting — those objects you find more often in a hotel room than a living room — *Boston, Philadelphia Today*, slicks of that ilk. But you would never guess, and the executives at Bean's didn't imagine, until it happened, which journal is Bean's all-time winner for buyers-gained-per-dollars-advertised: the *New York Review of Books*. That publication, strongly liberal, antiestablishment, given to essays of which books are the subject, often given over to lengthy correspondences between authors and reviewers that require the most exquisite reading and an attention span of weeks to keep the argument in mind, that magazine, due to its very educated and urban clientele (and its relatively low advertising rates) is the one. That is what it has come to — the person most in need of Maine Hunting Shoes and Maine Guide Shirts and Bean's Best Chamois Shirts is also the person who needs David Levine cartoons and endless discussions of neo-liberalism and the virtues of postmodern poetry. You figure it.

Bean's Employees: a Theory of the Working Class

ONE of the things that image-dependent companies do is check on their image — this is called "holding a focus group," or "having a focus group." The focusers are the marketing analysts and the customers are the focusees. A typical L. L. Bean story is about the focus group being had or held in Ohio, and the marketing man asked a lady in the group what she thought of when she thought of L. L. Bean. She responded, as if in a trance, "Oh, I see a small log cabin. There's a light in the window, and the snow is falling. It is so beautiful, so calm." Of course the lady knew that there was no log cabin. It was Abe Lincoln who was born in one, not L. L. Bean, Inc. Anyone who's paid any attention at all knows it was founded on the second floor of a downtown Freeport building, over the post office. And no one thinks that hundreds of millions of dollars' worth of goods are shipped from between peeled pine logs. Where they do come from, and how they are shipped, is somewhat less romantic, and better organized, than the lady ever imagined.

The L. L. Bean office, shipping warehouse, and factory, just south of Freeport, are the new, boring buildings on your right as you drive up Route 1 from Boston and Portland — the buildings with the big parking lot and the flags flying and the buildings with absolutely no sign that indicates you are passing the L. L. Bean, Inc. executive offices, warehouse, and factory. All you see from the outside are the tractor-trailer trucks: the ones on the south side are bringing in the goods, the ones on the north are shipping it out, the contract trucks for the U.S. Postal Service, the big, brown-cabbed rigs of the United Parcel Service. Generally speaking, there are just as many tractor-trailers on the north side as the south side, five days a week, fifty-two weeks a year. That is the organizational miracle that made the merchandising miracle of the Leon Gorman years possible. They call it turnover, and, when things grow right and go right, Bean is turning over its inventory on the average of six times a year — hot items, predictably hot items, may turn over as many as fifteen times a year. A truck of chamois cloth shirts comes in from Woolrich, and the delivery system trucks on the north side will be carrying as many away.

The Bean shipping system has a curious combination of workforce: the most modern of computer facilities running a hand- and foot-powered storage and retrieval system. Incredibly, as the business has grown to the point where Bean's is shipping over twenty million individual orders a year by 1983, a system that was supposed to handle a quarter of a million orders has kept pace. The secret has been computer planning, and a strict, paternal, and scientifically accurate system of rewards for productivity. There is no "speed-up" at L. L. Bean's, because there is no single, automatic, assembly line to be speeded up — what Bean's has done is speed up the individual workers.

Knowing how they did that will require understanding the whole system of picking and packing your order.

The interior of the 310,000-square-foot distribution center is two stories tall, with stock in two places — ready for picking and in reserve. Most of the reserve stock is high overhead the picking stock, accessible by high-rise forklift. The basic tool is the computer and the picking cart. The computer runs the entire operation; the function of the human worker is to set up, and fill, the picking cart, following exquisitely detailed instructions from the computer.

When an order comes in the mail or from the phone room, it is entered into the computer system by keypunchers, and if the computer agrees that the item is in stock, it buses the order to the shipping center. Most Bean orders are small, half of them for a single item, the average order just under two items.

The first thing the computer does is separate out the single-order items, and then re-sort them so that all the orders for a particular item — a tan chamois cloth shirt, for example — are in sequence. For particularly popular items, the computer will sort on, until all the size large tan chamois cloth shirts are in sequence. The reason is simple. When the Christmas rush hits, and the warehouse has forty-five thousand orders a day to fill, and six hundred pickers trying to fill them, there's an awfully good chance that a random distribution of orders to pickers would result in a hundred pickers descending on the chamois cloth shirt aisle at the same time.

Whether it is orders for single items, or multiple items, the computer selects the packing material — soft bag or cardboard box — to hold the order, and prints out a batch of orders to be picked that will exactly fill a single picking cart. The worker picks up his cart order, and the first task is to set up the cart. The picking cart has four shelves and opens on two sides. There are flip-up, flip-down partitions; each side of the cart can be four shelves, or thirty-two small compartments, eight to a shelf. The lucky picker that gets a cart order consisting entirely of small items will set up sixty-four compartments and proceed to one place, pick and fill, and move the cart to the packing stands, where it will be left, with the instructions as to packaging material, and the printouts of the mailing labels. A typical cart order will have ten to twelve compartments per side, twenty to forty for the whole cart. The cart layout is given to the picker in a visual form, a map of the next few minutes' work. In addition, the computer directs the picker to a particular parking area for the cart (the aisles of merchandise are too narrow to bring the carts to the goods) where the picker will leave the cart, sprint to the goods, and return. The computer will presort the orders, so, except in the slowest months when orders are fewest, the specific orders for a single cartload will mean the picker has to park the cart only once, and go down no more than two or three aisles to find his cartload of orders.

To watch the pickers at work is a study in the varieties of humankind. There are the head-down chargers and strollers, the quick and the slow. There are no dead. Good pickers average ninety orders (on the average of one hundred eighty items) an hour. But like everything at Bean's warehouse, speed is not enough. The same computer that plans order picking also keeps track of who picked it, and the error rate is calculated for every picker, every week.

At the packing stations, it is the same. Every shipment is keyed to the individual who packed it, and errors will be traced back, and the computer will know if the picker swapped the order, or the packer swapped the labels.

Judgment does not always wait for the customer to complain. The packers are expected to verify all the items selected by the picker, and supervisors pull packages randomly off the conveyor belt after packing, and open them, comparing the label to the packing list, the packing list to the contents, and the appropriateness of the size of the package to the contents. All errors are recorded. The employees know exactly what is going on. They are given a workload, and they know that there are weekly productivity reports, and weekly reports of errors they make.

None of the pickers and packers are, technically, on piecework wages, but all of them, except for the most inexperienced new hands, are paid on a basic scale with incentives for a high combination of speed and accuracy. Part-time employees (the warehouse staff triples in the fall rush) with experience at Bean's come back to a wage they established themselves in their previous part-time employment. The women standing at the packing desks, the men and women moving the picking carts, all have time to smile at a visitor, but their hands or their feet don't stop moving.

The computer system grows more sophisticated by the year, as the demands on the facility increase — it can order the shelf stockers to rearrrange the stock to minimize congestions — separating the most commonly ordered items, even separating the most common items by color or size, providing duplicate locations to keep the harried pickers from having to wait while someone else reaches in for a size large red chamois cloth shirt.

The same computer checks, thanks to the system that follows the order from incoming mail to the moment an automatic scale puts the right postage or USP fee on the package, means that everyone in the fulfillment system is also being watched, evaluated, and paid accordingly. Pure piecework is very rare at Bean's — the only ones on per-item payment are the moccasin-stitchers — that is an old tradition in the shoe business, and at Bean's. The old man could not have hired a decent shoemaker for his standard wage, the federal minimum plus a nickel. I asked a Bean executive once to point out their fastest moccasin-style-shoe-stitcher, and he nodded toward an older man with the typical bandaged fingers of a stitcher. "Used to be a high school principal," he told me, "but he could make more money sewing moccasins." He might make $22,000 a year — big money in the state of Maine.

No one should think that this system is grinding the faces of the poor, not by Maine terms. Other local industries (most of the shoe business having gone south, or across the Pacific Ocean) are hardly more attractive — you can fillet fish in Portland, or work the hot, fast-paced lines at B&M Baked Beans, or you can work one of the dozens of paper mills, toothpick mills, or small machining and plating businesses. Worst of all, you can try one of Maine's chicken-packing plants, and try and keep the conveyor belt loaded with chickens, grabbing them out of their shipping boxes at the rate of two every five seconds, or any of the worse jobs, farther down the line. The average turnover in a chicken-packing plant is 100 percent a month, if there's anywhere else to go.

The Old Man was proud of his low wages. "Many of our customers call here at Freeport," he wrote, ". . . some compare our prices with city prices for similar goods. I explain . . . that city stores are under a much greater expense. . . . We are located in a small town where living expense is at a minimum. Good wages here would be small in a city. Our prices are made accordingly."

The low wage scale in Maine still works to L. L. Bean's advantage, but it is the institutional paternalism of Leon

Gorman that makes the difference. If he knows the productivity of every factory and shipping employee, he is also paying a base wage 20 percent higher than other local factories. "In my view," he likes to say, "paying 20 percent above average in wages will get you a 30 to 40 percent above-average employee." And the supervisory system makes sure that you do. Bean also pays a share of Blue Cross insurance for the employees, and has a regular retirement program, unusual in the New England factories that tend to rely on Social Security to ease their consciences about their employees' retirement years. A typical Gorman device (though by no means his invention, it is just appropriate to his style) is a savings program — employees making long-term savings deposits, up to a certain percentage of their wages, get it matched, 25 cents on the dollar, by L. L. Bean, Inc.

The most remarkable part of Bean's employee benefit program is the annual bonus — a distribution of pre-tax profit to each full-time, and many of the seasonal, but regular, part-time employees. It is a percentage of your year's wages, or salary, and has averaged between 10 and 13 percent for the past several years. That is a flat percentage regardless of status, except as your status is reflected in your basic income.

Just as investment bankers and corporate acquisition officers eye Bean's with covetousness, so, too, a few unions have tried organizing the workers. Maine is not much of a union state, but the efforts at Bean's have been even less successful than elsewhere. The last union to try was the Teamsters, who managed to attract three of Bean's four-hundred-odd wage workers to a meeting.

As for the salaried workers, the hundred-odd managers' salaries are, apparently, comparable to Boston-area salaries, with the advantages of much lower real estate and construction costs. But, as one of them remarked, all the talk about country living and the good life is Maine is much exaggerated. "There is enormous pressure on us," he said. "We are caught between making the company grow and managing the growth so that we don't strangle on it. Everyone who came up here for the good life is gone."

The day he told me that, the company dismissed the manager of the retail store — a store that was turning out incredible sales, averaging $800 per square foot annually, two and three times the square-foot return in a typical department store. The popularity of the store had forced a major expansion and renovation (more carpeting, more fake barn boards on the walls) and the store manager just wasn't up to speed, in Leon Gorman's terms, on managing the renovations.

If Bean's can run its own show, internally, at top speed and minimum cost, that does not really solve the problems of rapid growth. Most of their products, 80 to 85 percent, are purchased from outside, including all the men's and women's clothing — categories that account for well over half their annual business in dollar terms. A few of the outside items are brand-labeled, and of known, nationally approved quality — Pendleton wool shirts, Bass shoes, Coleman stoves and lanterns. But the rest, almost 75 percent of their catalog items, have no reputation except Bean's name, and quality control, until 1981, was nonexistent.

Buying clothing, as any honest mail-order or department store buyer will admit, is the most difficult and occasionally unpleasant of tasks. The garment industry is basically run on an "as per sample" basis, and, too often, when the goods arrive, the methods of stitching and the quality of the material has suffered a change — not for nothing do shoppers become brand-name and designer-name conscious. As the business continued to double and triple in the years from 1965 to 1980, there was a fall-off in quality in some items, that even Leon Gorman will admit. One of the funniest, and least costly in the long run, was the unhappy debut of an item of fishing tackle. For years, L. L. Bean had sold, at best, middle-of-the-road fishing tackle. Then, in 1978, they decided it was time to go upscale and join the others, and they started looking for a fancy flyrod made with graphite fibers. "Graphite" is a somewhat misleading term for carbonized polyster fibers — a very strong material of very light weight that was developed in Great Britain as a modern aerodynamic material. It is used in profusion in jet fighters, today, and in some quantity in the manufacture of fishing rods and golf club shafts. Bean's went to what may best be described as a very reputable Vermont fishing tackle manufacturer and ordered a series of rods. Unfortunately, the very reputable manufacturer did shoddy work, and Bean's ended up refunding practically every customer's money — the wire guides on the rods came loose almost instantly. Since then, in fly-fishing matters, they have changed manufacturers and brought a nationally known angler, Dave Whitlock, on board as a consultant in rod design.

The problems in clothing and sleeping bags were less spectacular than denuded fishing rods, but equally frustrating. Colors faded, cloth abraded, and some down was adulterated. The response was the development of a full-scale materials testing laboratory, housed on the mezzanine of the shipping warehouse. Clothes are washed and dried, machinery repeatedly pokes or rubs material until it begins to show signs of wear, down fibers are pulled out of clothing and sleeping bags, and the down is weighed and examined microscopically. This is not 100-percent testing, but still, a conscientious sampling of all incoming goods. Curiously, for so large a sales operation, Bean still does not create specifications for its products — it may specify the type of down (there are several kinds, and U.S. government definitions; prime northern waterfowl, prime waterfowl, and waterfowl are the three highest categories, in that order), but it seldom goes so far as to specify the thread used for seams and buttons, or the exact type of weave in the material — it remains an "as per sample" business. In that respect, it is not unlike the little log cabin general store in the Ohio lady's mind — Bean's is still locked in to the world of salesmen and manufacturers' representatives.

Of course, the real quality-control system is the customer, who returns about 5 percent of everything ordered from L. L. Bean, and Leon Gorman, who has the computer data to prove it, says that 95 percent of the goods returned are for "customer preference" — there's nothing particularly wrong with it, it's just the color or the shape or whatever. The return policy remains what it always claimed to be, no reason needed, no excuse required, no abuse of the article too strong to justify refusing a refund. It was, in fact, not always so. Bean's 100-percent guarantee was not always extended to customers who had obviously abused an item beyond any reasonable wear and tear — shirts returned with great chlorine bleach blotches on them, or shoes with knife or saw cuts through the leather, or dog's teeth marks clearly visible. Certain customers, after several abuses, have been put on notice, particularly a family from Machiasport, Maine, who were in the habit of constantly returning Maine Hunting Shoes scavenged from the dump, and claiming a full refund, but you have to go some to upset even the computerized customer service department at Bean's.

"I have trouble explaining the return policy to some of

our business visitors," Gorman told me. "There is no return policy." It was during L.L.'s declining years that company employees began to exercise a little independent judgment, arguing with the customer about the reality of his claims. One of Gorman's first jobs at Bean, after he had taken over his father's job as clothing buyer, was the retail store. "When I took it over," he said, "one of the biggest problems was when somebody would bring back something that had obviously been abused, and the store clerk would take it as a personal matter, that the customer was taking advantage of the company, and the clerk. So, he'd bring the thing back to me, and we'd argue about whether to give a 50-percent refund, or 75, whatever." He snapped his hand as if to brush away a particularly annoying black fly. "I finally got that stopped."

The cost of this generous return policy is enormous — and one of the serious problems yet unsolved. About 5 percent of the goods are returned, the company says, although 6 percent is an unofficial figure that is closer to the apparent truth. That sounds like a small percentage, but 5 percent of some $240 million worth of goods, goods averaging $12 per item, is 1.2 million pieces of merchandise to be checked in, stored, and resold. It is crushing the company's ability to react. The most likely way to deal with the returns (a fraction can be sold in the discount room at the Freeport store, and some goods are showing up in discount stores outside of Maine) is to open a return store somewhere else, a long way from Freeport.

Customer service is housed in the same headquarters buildings on Route 1, and if they do not have to spend much time worrying about a return policy, they do spend considerable time (a full-time staff of forty, with many dozens more during the Christmas rush) answering customers' questions. And the basic question, in spite of every effort, is "Where's my order?" The arithmetic is pretty simple: fiscal 1983 sales of $237 million included some $200 million in mail order, and 4.8 million separate orders. Even Bean's vaunted policy of having 90 percent of the goods in stock when the order arrives, shipping the next 5 percent within twenty-one days, and failing to ship only 5 percent makes for a tremendous workload.

The average order is 1.9 items, so that Bean's $240 million in 1984 generated orders for some 9.12 million separate items — at a 10 percent out-of-stock rate, that's nearly one million missing items, nearly half a million customers that need to be notified. After twenty-one days, there are still a quarter of a million customers waiting for nearly half a million items that have to be offered a refund, or advised to keep waiting. And a quarter of a million people with access to a telephone and a complaint in their hearts is a lot of business to handle in even a forty-person customer relations department. It is no wonder that there is no toll-free number for calling L. L. Bean, let alone a toll-free number for their customer service department.

Both customer service and telephone order, housed in the anonymous administration building south of town, are staffed by local residents, 99 percent married women, who have made a career of being nice on the telephone. Both are prized jobs at L. L. Bean's, with convenient hours, flexible for the part-timers and Christmas rush fill-ins, and they pay unusually well for what is, by normal office standards, nonskilled work. But what Bean demands, and gets, is unwavering loyalty to the company's goals of complete service and an imperturbable friendly manner in the face of customer rudeness. The rules are simple: never get mad, never hang up, and listen out the problem. If all else fails, encourage the customer to write, and shift into that cooler medium of communication.

The computer that drives the ordering, picking, and packing system is available both to order takers (who can tell the customer whether the item is currently in stock) and to customer service representatives who can, once the order is entered in the system, tell the customer whether it is in the process of being picked, or packed, or exactly when it was shipped. More powerfully, the computer can shortstop the calls to customer service by deluging the delayed customer with regular, computer-written notices of when the item is expected to be available for shipping. It is a most peculiar mixture, like most of the company, of the most modern and powerful computational ability and genuine personableness. "One of the reasons we decided not to go to toll-free calls," a customer service executive told me, "is that the customers spend so much time just chatting with the girls when it's *their* nickel. We don't mind talking about the weather up here, but I think it would get out of hand with a free telephone line."

By and large, the L. L. Bean employee is happy in his or her work. More than once, at indoctrination meetings for new employees, I have heard them explain, in answer to a standard question, why they wanted to work at L. L. Bean — "Because the last place I worked sold junk. . . . Because the last place I worked treated customers like dirt, like they weren't even there. . . . Because I wanted to work for a place that had some pride in what it sold." It is quite genuine, and when the feeling ever goes away, the computer and the supervisors are there to notice that you've lost the urge to play the game by Leon Gorman's rules.

The
Limits of Growth

M ANAGING growth in mail-order sales remained Bean's
most serious problem for a dozen years, until Leon
Gorman deliberately slowed Bean's annual growth to a
leisurely 5 percent in fiscal 1984. When growth exceeded
expectations, the problems of out-of-stock merchandise
began to put sand in the otherwise smooth gears. Bean's
has kept its systems up to coping with the growth, and now
the customer service department sends out computerized
sorry-about-that notices every ten days to expectant customers. The company insists that they have 90 percent of
the goods on hand, when ordered, and are able to deliver
half of the out-of-stock within ten days — but that is 90
percent of the stock-keeping-units ordered by customers,
not necessarily 90 percent of customers' orders — a single
popular item, when its sales are grossly underestimated,
may be out of stock for weeks on end.

The current rule is that mail-order companies must offer to refund the customer's money if it can't ship goods
within twenty-one days. It is called the "Alaska Sleeping

Bag Company Rule" in the mail-order trade, after that long-defunct company that offered good value but couldn't deliver the goods. At one point in the late 1960s, Alaska Sleeping Bag accounted for fully 90 percent of all the complaints sent to the Federal Trade Commission. Alaska Sleeping Bag's problems were of their own making. If Bean's had three colors of chamois shirts, ASB would offer a dozen colors. The trade name for all the sizes and varieties of product in a store is "stock-keeping-unit" (SKUs), a more useful indication of how many things you've got to worry about than product names. Bean's is up to around twenty thousand SKUs, partly able to hold back by pretending that there are no women in the world smaller than size 8. (Even Preppies run to smaller sizes than that, although the average female Preppie, if Dartmouth undergraduates are a good example, run to size 12 and up.) Bean's is not alone in ignoring the smaller woman, among the trendy catalogs — Orvis women's clothes almost never drop below size 8 — on the other hand, both carry size 5 shoes. But admitting that the world had size 4, 5, and 6 women in it would move up Bean's SKUs on the order of several hundred items.

The worst year, in the past twelve, for underestimating the rate of growth in sales was 1981. There was a substantial business turndown that year, a mini-recession, and Bean's forecast a modest growth rate (for them) of only 25 percent in sales, following four years when sales increases were over 30 percent annually. What Bean's did not understand, in spite of all their market research, is that their customers are not, by and large, affected by a business recession. With over two-thirds of their customers holding a bachelor's degree, and another third being graduate-level professionals of one kind or another, they had no reason actually to fear a slowdown. Accordingly, to keep their predicted sales up to 25 percent, unmindful of the actual disposable income of their true customers, Bill End and his associates increased their direct-mail expenses from $2.6 million in 1980 to $3.6 million in 1981. Direct-mail expense covers everything from the cost of printing and mailing catalogs, to the expense of advertising for new customers and rentals of other companies' mailing lists. This was a 38-percent increase in direct-mail costs over fiscal 1980, which they thought would give them a 20-percent increase in the number of buyers. Inflation in the cost of goods, and therefore the size of the average order, would, they thought, give them their 25-percent growth from that 20-percent increase in buyers. Theoretically, they would get an average order of $54.70 in 1981, compared to the $50.67 average order of 1980.

They were wrong. It became apparent early in the fall that they would not be able to handle the anticipated rush of orders for Christmas. The one valve they had that could shut down the flow of orders was the same one that they had used for the previous five years to increase orders — change the number of catalogs they mailed. Although the major fall catalog was out in the mails when the predictions of the impending flood were made, Bean's still had 9 million Christmas catalogs sitting at the printers. They calculated that the 9 million catalogs would generate about $20 million worth of business if they were sent to the company's best list of names. (As of 1981, Bean's had about 1.4 million buying customers out of about 10 million names it was mailing catalogs to.) They held back a million and a half Christmas catalogs, and waited for the tide of orders to ebb.

But sitting there with $420,000 worth of four-color printing on slick paper bothered Leon Gorman's sense of thrift, and, after consultations, Bean's decided to send the one and a half million Christmas catalogs to a list, as they told me, of their "worst" customers — people who hadn't ordered for years, or who didn't order up to the $50 standard of a good customer. That is what they said they were doing, and it had a most undesirable effect. The Christmas catalog mailing, whether to preferred customers or "worst" customers, produced an avalanche of orders in 1981, and the business grew by 40 percent anyway.

I believed that whole story at the time, when it was explained to me. The idea of mailing a catalog to old customers who hadn't ordered for years seemed like a reasonable way to generate a little business, but not too much. That is what they told me they were doing, and it seemed to make sense. On reflection, either they were kidding themselves, or they were kidding me. Bill End, when he started at Bean's in 1975, tried a number of methods for increasing sales, and one of them should have told him what would happen when he tried mailing to "worst" customers. When he arrived, there was already in place a "master file" of L. L. Bean customers, not a mailing list of prospects, but actual buyers. And that was purged every three years, eliminating the names of people who had not bought anything. Of all the lists of names Bill End tried in his first few years at Bean's, be it another company's customer list or names gathered from advertisements, customer referrals, or the sign-up sheets in the factory store, the list of former buyers was the best: "We found this 'rejuvenated' segment," he said, "to be by far the best list we tested [in 1976]." It should not have surprised them that sending a million and a half catalogs to persons who had formerly, or were currently, buying from Bean's, would generate considerable business. Whether the "worst customer" mailing was a genuine mistake — resulting in unexpectedly great pressure on operations and customer service — or whether it was an in-house ploy to boost sales without giving operations and customer service executives a chance to object, is moot. It was a long time ago, and no one can really remember, anymore.

The one thing that is true about the growth of L. L. Bean, Inc., is that no matter how hard they worked to make the company grow, it still surprised them when it grew so rapidly. They were riding a tiger, up there in Freeport, and they wondered at its strength and speed.

As the "unintentional" 40-percent growth showed in 1981, the Gorman/End rules still applied after a decade: the more catalogs you mail, the more orders you get. When Leon Gorman, faced with the necessity of either slowing growth, nearly stopping it, in fiscal 1983–84, it was easy to do: catalog mailings dropped, and he was able to avoid building a new warehouse in Freeport.

What to do, now that the growth in retail sales has been slowed, is the major decision that Leon Gorman faces. There were strong indications that the rate of growth was slowing down, that the traditional formulas that matched customers with products were less and less powerful solutions.

The rental of mailing lists was beginning to pall as a source of buyers — in the late 1970s rented lists were bringing in a quarter of Bean's new customers each year, keeping pace with company goals. But that system began to lag toward the end of the decade. As an example, the response rate (actual goods ordered) from rented mailing lists was 2.98 percent in 1978, and had declined to 2.25 percent in 1981 — 2.25 percent would make most mail-order houses happy, but when Leon Gorman saw a decline of 32 percent in the response rate, he knew he was looking at the future. Declines like that, and declines in the response to newspaper and magazine advertisements, were raising marketing costs — list rental and advertising costs took less than 12 percent of the annual gross income of the company in 1978, and the same costs were rising past the 15-percent mark by 1983 — the expense in dollars was just under $7 million in 1978, and had soared to over $33 million in the 1983 fiscal year.

The cause of the shift was obvious — by 1981, Bean catalogs were being mailed to a third of all American households that bought clothing or footwear by mail. Even more serious was the demographic reach — Bean's was reaching 50 percent of the footwear and clothing buyers with incomes over $25,000 in 1981. The drop in response to advertising and mail-order rental lists was sharp, and reflected in the total number of new buyers — in 1977, when the hottest rental lists were used for the first time, after extensive sampling of those lists in 1976, buyer growth was 32 percent over the previous year. By 1980, once Bean had run through the Orvis, the Eddie Bauer, the W. Atlee Burpee Seed Company, and all the other good lists, new buyer growth was down to 8 percent, and company growth was clearly dependent on getting old customers to spend more on each order. Given the gender of the new customers added by list rental and advertising — they were at least 70 percent female — that would mean, would demand, adding even more products for the women in Bean's life.

The year 1980 also saw a disturbing drop in a special category of new customers — the so-called unknowns, the ones that could not be traced back to a specific advertisement, mailing list, or into Bean's own records. An "unknown" can arise from any of a dozen sources, or problems in the system — customers who don't add the phony street address or phony box number that would allow them to be tagged to a single magazine advertisement are a major source of unknowns; so are people who forget to use the pull-off, stick-on preprinted mailing label on their order form. All of those preprinted labels are coded to show which of many rented lists, or Bean lists, the customer is on. Bean still gets large numbers of orders on plain paper — which makes them impossible to trace. Someone will borrow a catalog, for example, after the order form has been used. Follow-ups on the "unknowns" indicate that perhaps half of them are genuine new buyers. The rest are just folks who got themselves lost in the Bean computer — having changed address, or forgotten to use the preprinted labels. But that 50 percent who are genuine new customers, people who found L. L. Bean before Bean found them, were terribly important indicators of the general public's awareness of, affection for, and interest in L. L. Bean. And the number of "unknown" new buyers was the single category that did not continue to grow from 1977 onward — beginning in 1980, new buyers that could not be traced to specific sources actually declined each year — another indication that the universe of people who would ever buy from L. L. Bean had already been discovered, identified, and sent a catalog.

Still there are millions more potential customers out there, as Leon Gorman would say, "and we have an obligation to bring our products to the people. As long as we can deliver value to society," he continued, "we are obliged to do it."

The places to look for these new buyers seemed obvious — the booming Sun Belt South and the Pacific Coast. Bean's is fairly successful at selling Maine Hunting Shoes to southern trappers and crawfish snaggers, but it hasn't penetrated Dixie's upscale homes. The central South, west of the Appalachians, from Knoxville to New Orleans, has 6.5 percent of the U.S. population, but provides Bean with only 3.9 percent of its customers. The company does even worse in the Southwest, from Texas to Arizona, where 10.5 percent of the U.S. population turns up only 4.5 percent of the company's buyers. These figures were even worse when Bill End started tuning up the rental list system and expanding the company's advertising. But although Bean shows slow growth west of the Appalachians, it clearly has not penetrated the West — after all kinds of efforts, including using the locally popular Eddie Bauer list, and local advertising, Bean's gets less than 10 percent of its customers from the Pacific states, and those three states are growing to the point where they hold 15 percent of the nation's households.

More ominous were the clear signs of market saturation in the New England states and the New York megalopolis — the New England and Mid-Atlantic states provided 45 percent of Bean's 700,000 customers in 1976. By 1981, they provided only 40 percent of the customers. The absolute number of buyers in the Northeast did increase, from about 322,000 to 577,000, an 80-percent increase in five years, but the company's growth in customers overall was 110 percent, and near 120 percent in other geographical areas. Market saturation, like rust on an automobile, begins with almost imperceptible little disfigurements on the body.

As Bean's peaked out in the East, and grew slowly in the rest of the country, it had, still has, many options for continued growth — many places to put its net income, approaching $30 million a year in 1984. Flogging the mailing lists is perhaps the least useful investment, as the problem of saturation becomes clear. But, continue to grow it must, or start to lose some of the bright young souls that have made the company so successful. Even worse, those bright young folks might start to slow down, something that bothered Leon Gorman, as he said: "We'd lose some commitment." Bill End was more specific. "There are people here would leave tomorrow," he told Harvard researchers, "if they thought we were going to plateau at current sales levels."

In the spring of 1983, the year they started to plateau, the vice-president for marketing took a long look at this decision to slow down, and walked out the door. Long before the slowdown, two of Bean's managers were arguing about how long the growth could last, how long they could grow without a fundamental change in the product line and the customer profile. "I'll tell you one thing," the marketing man said to the product man, "there aren't enough Preppies in the world for this company to keep growing." It was 1983–84 when they ran out of Preppies, it was 1983–84 when Leon Gorman decided, perhaps only temporarily, not to go looking for that fundamentally different customer, decided not to further alter the product line, and the image, of L. L. Bean.

The options for the future are still there, particularly overseas. Leon Gorman occasionally thinks that there is a whole world to conquer. "It is clear," he told me, that marketing surveys in other countries, "including Canada, England and Japan, show that the Bean name, like Pepsi, has at least a temporary value." For America, after all, is not the mail-order capital of the world, in spite of Sears, Montgomery-Ward, and their imitators. Americans spend only 2.5 percent of their retail purchase money by mail. In Great Britain, mail order gets more than twice as large a share, 5.3 percent of all retail. West Germans spend almost 5 percent by mail. France, Italy, the Netherlands, and Switzerland, although new to the whole concept of mail order, are showing annual growth rates of 20 percent and more in the share, however tiny the beginning, of purchases by mail. Mail order in Great Britain in quite understandable, particularly in durable goods — there is a tradition in hardware, sporting goods, and home appliances of retail stores of carrying tiny inventories, so that visiting the store is merely a chance to look at the object itself, and you will, in effect, have to order by mail in the long run. The problems with exporting merchandise, particularly into the European Common Market Countries and Canada, are enormous, as the consumer has to make his own customs payments, usually at the main post office, sometimes even at the port of entry — it is a deliberate slowdown by the local government, a bureaucratic imposition of import quotas by delay and frustration.

To date, although Bean's still ships to the whole world, the only retail outlet outside of Freeport, Maine, is in Japan. Bean has an agreement with Sony to carry selected Bean items, and sell them in a few of Sony's retail stores. (All the Japanese electronic and appliance manufacturers sell directly to the public through company-owned stores — and these stores, carefully monitored by the company, provide a great deal of their information on customer preferences. They are marketing devices, as well as profit centers.) But the Sony stores allocate only small corners to Bean products, and the retail costs are at least twice U.S. costs. The items are fairly predictable, particularly Maine Hunting Shoes in the low-cut styles appropriate for street wear, and men's clothing. But Sony does import some real sporting goods, fishing tackle items like the Arcticreel for Japan's millions of fishermen, and duck decoys (even in that crowded country, duck hunting is possible). But given the network of legal and administrative barriers to export of consumer goods, Bean's is unlikely to become a major exporter.

The most obvious, and the safest, least upsetting to the

image, manner of growth will be to expand the company's manufacturing capacity. If you take away the shoes it makes (all of the Maine Hunting Shoe styles and most of the moccasin-style footwear) Bean's makes far less than 10 percent of the other goods it sells — besides footwear, it manufactures the simpler canvas items, bags and wood carriers, and some very simple leather goods, particularly belts. Belts, as anyone knows who walked the streets of San Francisco at the height of the Flower Child era, are something that anyone can make. But, then, anyone can make shoes, too. Bean has been able to sell some shoes to other retailers — it has manufactured moccasin-style loafers for the Orvis fishing tackle company for the past several years.

Another possibility, a very nervous-making one, is to expand the retail store business. Bean has actually sold goods over the counter outside of Freeport on one occasion — they hired an empty storefront in Boston, near the Old Burying Ground, for one Christmas season. But the Freeport store remains a trademark of the company, a mecca, a destination for customers who can, for once in their life, see and touch everything in the catalog. Moving away from Freeport makes Leon Gorman very nervous. Even though the Freeport store averages $900 per square foot (at least four times the annual sales per square foot of the nation's most successful department stores), Leon Gorman was not kidding when he said: "I don't think we know much about running a retail store." The growth of business in the store (it will do about $40 million in 1984) is a function of the number of mail-order buyers the catalog can generate. It has no independent magic formula.

Bean's is besieged with requests from the major department store chains, Affiliated, Federated, Macy's, and Gimbel's, to move into their stores. Bean's is offered whole floors to install what would become a sort of L. L. Bean boutique, matching the kinds of spaces that stores now allocate to designer clothes. Bill End listened to the offers, and rejected thm "because of our strong growth in the mail-order business *and the risk of L. L. Bean's image*." Leon Gorman, who worries about Bean's image as much as anyone, has other reasons. "I know of no company that has successfully distributed both ways," he told the Harvard Business School. "As Bauer and Talbots have concentrated on retail, their catalog marketing has suffered. The two approaches require very different kinds of management. Mail-order marketers are very analytic, quantitatively oriented. Retailers have to be creative, promotional, pizzazy, merchandise oriented. It's tough to assemble one management team that can handle both functions."

Still, Bean's continues to study the possibilities of moving retail out of Freeport — watching Bauer (which has a dozen retail stores, coast-to-coast, added after it was purchased by the Quaker Oats company) and Oshman's Sporting Goods, a Houston-based mail-order and sporting goods store chain. Oshman's sells everything from guns to gewgaws, most of them through "fun stores" targeted at the upscale consumer in the Sun Belt: Alabama, Arizona, Florida, Georgia, Louisiana, Tennessee, and Texas. If Oshman's had no cachet equivalent to L. L. Bean's, they managed to buy a name with cachet — paying the bankrupt Abercrombie & Fitch for the company name and logo. Oshman's has added several A&F stores since 1977, and began mailing an Abercrombie & Fitch Catalog in 1979. It is, of course, competing with itself. Oshman's, Bauer, Orvis, and the rest of Bean's competitors in mail order are growing much more slowly than Bean's. Oshman's is doing the best, with a compounded growth rate around 20 percent, but with a much more burdensome investment in real estate. Oshman's stores sell about $140 per square foot — not bad, but not Bean, either.

The most intriguing idea for Bean, one they are studying constantly in the 1980s, is to take their management expertise in mail-order marketing and apply it to another type of catalog. They could purchase, or start up, a completely noncompetitive mail-order business — men's dress clothes, for example, or electronics and appliances. Rather than see their company swallowed by a conglomerate, like every other major mail-order retailer, Bean's might do a little swallowing of its own, and become, as it were, a conglomerate giant of the mailing-list industry. But whatever they do, grow they must. It is the rule of life in business, even if L. L. Bean, himself, got tired of growing for growth's sake. The sudden stop in growth that characterized 1983–1984 was a conscious decision, but a temporary one.

An Uncertain Future

I N the folk story of Paul Bunyan, that giant logger who was born and brought up in Maine, there is a description of the year of the blue snow. It was so cold that the birdsong froze solid the minute the beak was opened. No one in the logging camp in the north woods could hear a word that was said outdoors, no matter how loudly even Paul Bunyan shouted, as the words froze the moment they were said and dropped to the hard blue snow without even a faint tinkling sound to mark their fall. Come spring, and the thaw, the noise was deafening, a mad rush of twitters and bellows and shouts of "timber," all mingled in the soft air.

The winter of 1983–1984 was the time of the blue snow for L. L. Bean, Inc. After twenty years of uninterrupted growth, and after five years, from 1978 to 1983, of spectacular growth, everything froze. Gross sales stood near their 1982–1983 level, some $230 million, and this in a spectacular year for general merchants, when purchasing by American consumers ran 10 percent over 1982.

It was the year something happened, and not even the

people at L. L. Bean are sure what it was that abruptly, in a time of general economic improvement, stopped their company dead in the water. The simplest explanation, one that may turn out to be true when springtime comes to L. L. Bean's country and the words unfreeze, is that they ran out of Preppies. Virtually every household in America that might buy gear by mail is currently inundated with clothing catalogs, some of them so clearly ripped off the mold of L. L. Bean that Bean's onetime uniqueness is now just another piece of slick paper. The company's crusty attitude toward products, their very slow introduction of new colors, new styles, had left them miles behind their real competitors — Land's End, J. Crew, and that ilk of merchandise. A Bean's sweater came in one or two colors, women's outerwear remained bulky, but not fashionably, not outrageously, oversized. It was almost impossible, leafing through a Bean catalog, to say aloud, "That's cute," or "That's handsome." You might say, "That's durable," but that is the kind of phrase that can easily be repressed, it does not spring unbidden to the lips.

And the method of success may have taken its toll — the repetitive mailings have interrupted the very seasonality that linked Bean's with the great outdoors, the old, pawky, spring book that arrived when the lakes were still frozen in Preppie land, let alone in the big woods of Maine, the fall book that came in the heat of August and promised leaf color and the smell of damp woods, a book that fairly reeked of apple time, as the spring book somehow seemed full of strawberry. Now they pour in, spring, winter, summer, fall, Christmas, and small books that appear unbidden in October or April, nine a year to most customers, a dozen a year to the better customers, six hundred pages of the same things, the same look, the same sensibility.

Leon Gorman, underneath his smiling protestations that Bean's had not yet brought its products to every American, has always known that someday the growth could stop, or slow to that snail's pace that amounts to the same thing. And he has always insisted that when the character of the company, when its styles, its product line, its customers, required some major changes to maintain that growth, he would not sacrifice the company's essential character to maintain the heady pace of the 1970s and early 1980s. His decision to slow down in 1983–1984 was not explained to his staff, not talked out in meetings. "Leon looked at all the numbers," an insider remarked, "but it wasn't the numbers. He makes intuitive decisions, and he decided that he didn't like what he saw happening to the company."

The growth, however, stopped too soon to save the essential character of two things — the L. L. Bean Factory Store on Main Street, and the ambiance of Freeport, a sleepy village now firmly in the twentieth century. Even McDonald's, although without the Golden Arches, has come to Freeport, and it is all the doing of Leon Gorman, Bill End, and the two and a half million customers that trek each year to Freeport.

Two and a half million people go to a lot of places in the East, the Cape Cod National Seashore visitors' center on Cape Cod, downtown Lake Placid, New York, now the site of two winter Olympic Games, the baseball hall of fame in Cooperstown, New York. But Freeport is different. We're talking about two and half million people who have come to a sleepy town of six thousand residents with money to spend on retail goods. And the results are predictable.

For years, the state of Maine tried to figure out how to get tourists to spend money on something more than food and lodging. Maine promoted retail outlets for local industries, shoes, shirts, and moccasins for the largest part, and they encouraged boutique outlets convenient to the Maine Turnpike, the artery that bears five million tourists a year up the road from Boston to Portland and farther on to the down east coast and up to the north woods. What the office of tourism and development could not do, Bean's could do — it could provide a single site in one of the largest and least populated states of the nation, close to the Eastern megalopolis, where the dollar-bringing tourists could be ambushed by every upscale retailer in the world.

For now, the second largest retail store in Freeport, Maine, is a Ralph Lauren outlet, a block south of the Bean store. And the Dansk Design Company, after floundering for a few years off Exit One of the Maine Pike, has moved into what was once Leighton's Five and Dime, a store once filled with things that only looked good to small children on small allowances. There is upscale lingerie at Barbizon, what appears to be a quarter-acre of Hathaway shirts, and a Cole-Hahn bootery in which, as Mrs. George Soule remarked drolly, "you can find something nice for less than $200."

There are, for 1984, twenty-five permits for new retail stores under consideration at the town planning board. Every one of those stores is hoping to skim something off the traffic generated by Bean's store, and that store opened a massive addition on Memorial Day, 1984. About a year earlier, the town's last grocery store closed. There is no money in canned goods in Freeport, unless they're the little cans of camp food you can pick up at L. L. Bean, Inc., where the founder once fulminated against selling anything that smacked of a souvenir.

But these are merely the changes of scale, and the addition of new players to the money game. The more fundamental change, the final change, inside the big "factory store" was the day the sales clerks started wearing their blue shirts with the neatly stenciled "L. L. Bean" over the pocket, the day the clerks started to look like waiters and waitresses in one of those polyurethane-covered-wooden-table-and-Boston-fern-bedecked restaurants that appear in every abandoned brick building in North America — the kind of restaurants that have two varieties of pickled mushrooms in the salad bar containers.

There is a version of that sort of restaurant right across the side street from the new addition to the factory store, the restored Jameston Tavern with a glossy bar and waitresses who tell you their name before they disappear on more urgent business. There are no retired game wardens waiting on customers in the store, or ordering steaks at the Jameson Tavern. The young ones, the jaded-eyed youth you see everywhere, the ones wearing their employer's name over their heart, have taken over.

Souvenirs abound in the factory store, when once it was the very anonymity of an L. L. Bean piece of clothing that nearly shouted its origin. Their denim and corduroy jeans, piled high on the counters, have adapted the leather patch, the brand-name patch, the leather patch on the waistband over the right hip pocket, to advertise the origin of the pants, pants that were once recognized by their fullness at the crotch and their untapered legs, because the L. L. Bean leather patch, unlike the classic Levi's patch, is only sewn along the top and the bottom, and you can use it as an extra belt loop and run your belt underneath it and become an advertisement of yourself and of L. L. Bean, even in Cleveland. There are L. L. Bean beach towels, the letters large enough to be read by a normal human eye from a quarter mile away. There is the L. L. Bean ski bag, letters that stand out on cars roaring up the turnpikes, headed for the ski hills. And now the Bean boat bag, that canvas object that was actually developed for carrying ice, not ice to the refrigerator in a three-decker, but ice to the refrigerator in a yacht, even that bag now says L. L. Bean on it. There is no mystique left in the canvas ice bag, you can buy canvas ice bags in every major city in America.

One should not be too cynical about souvenirs, not even the red candy lobsters that you can buy in the factory store. All shrines sell souvenirs, be they portraits of the saint or printed prayers. Bean's has evolved to that now, it is a destination, there is the pilgrimage up the Maine Pike and there is, still, that sense of liminality, of crossing a threshold, when you enter the store. It is not about to be destroyed by a few souvenirs, any more than Notre Dame is tarnished because you can purchase a color transparency of the rose window.

It will be fascinating, for students of retailing, to watch what happens on Main Street, Freeport, in the next few years. The assumption that two and a half million people will come to town with money and plastic cards does not prove that other retailers will be so successful as Bean's. Anyone who is cynical about the power and the magic of L. L. Bean has only to stand in one of the parking lots to be swiftly disabused of the notion that Bean's is just another successful retail store.

Is there another store in America where people stop at their automobile in the parking lot and take the clothes and the gear out of the bags and look at it one more time before packing it into the trunk? They show it to each other, they laugh, they chat feverishly about it, more like children comparing report cards after school than like consumers who have just spent a week's pay on gear. There are at least as many women as men, most of them young and healthy-looking, as though they had just finished doing their barre exercises, or just put away their squash rackets.

Several times, without loitering, but just while passing through the lots or along the metered parking on Main Street, I have seen a man, usually a young man, but no mere lad, always alone, stop at his automobile and take off his jacket, whatever sort of jacket, a suit coat or a down parka, and open his L. L. Bean paper bag and take out a genuine L. L. Bean flight jacket, the dark brown leather one, the one with the mouton collar and the zippered pocket on the sleeve, and put it on. And all of this happened before there was a movie called *The Right Stuff*.

What you are watching, it becomes clear, is a love affair with a merchant being acted out on the sidewalks and in the parking lot. Yes, it is good merchandise, yes it is a good value, but good things at the right price are available in so many places. That is not what is going on here in Freeport, this is different. This is donning the pilgrim's clothes, this is wearing the outward and visible sign of some interior and invisible grace. It would be laughable, if it were some particular garment that is famous for fifteen weeks, something like a rugby shirt or a Gucci tie. But these people are not donning fads — L. L. Bean has sold leather aviator's jackets since the end of World War II. It has only been in the past year that everyone sells them, only in the past year that you got advertisements for them with your American Express bill.

The only thing I have ever seen like it, a sight even remotely approaching what you can see every day in Freeport, was a group of French nationals, tourists, who descended on a clothing store in Rawlings, Wyoming, and emerged a half hour later in Levi's, western shirts with pearl buttons on the cuffs and pockets, latigo vests and three and a half inch brim Stetsons. They, too, had that same merriment, that same sense of having arrived, that sense of joining, of merging with the myth, in their case, of Henry Fonda and Jack Palance and John Wayne. It was a gaudier show, in downtown Rawlings, and one more mythically freighted, carrying a deeper burden of assimilation and conversion, but, somehow, not unlike the donning of the aviator's jacket, not so dissimilar from taking the pins out of the chamois cloth shirt, the one that Mr. Bean wore on all his hunting and fishing expeditions, and pulling the shirt on over your old clothing, wearing it outside the waistband, wearing it like a jacket. A jacket, and a badge of membership.

Whether that lure that draws the two and a half million to Freeport will rub off on Ralph Lauren and Hathaway and the twenty-five new stores about to open is problematical. It is true that the same people who buy at Bean's, by and large, do buy funny little polo shirts with horses on them, drink coffee out of Danish crockery, wear Hathaway shirts, these people do all those things you do if you went to college and got a job. But that does not mean that the same motives that lure them to Freeport will make them cross the street and buy Italian shoes.

One way to look at loyal Bean customers is to define the customers, real or potential, as belonging to one or another particular class. One class is that blend of education, status, social training, and avocations that make up what we have loosely called Preppies, understanding that Preppie gear is, and always has been, for sale in every cow college town as well as along the Eastern Seaboard. And the second of these two groups is what vice-president Bill End calls "hardcore outdoor jocks." Those are definitions that depend on the customer's self image, on the desire to be part of one of those two groups, in a smaller number of cases, to be part of both groups, not only to be a Preppie, or an outdoor jock, but to be both at once, which, loosely speaking, makes you a Sport. If that is all that an L. L. Bean customer is, or wishes to be, then two things are understandable. The first is the sudden slowdown in the growth of the company, when, finally, it had reached some large percentage, if not 100 percent, of all the potential old-style customers that were out there, waiting for a catalog. The second is that all those upscale shops are correct in their decision to build outlets across Main Street from the Mother Store. They will have to find out if it is possible to turn Preppies, in *Time* magazine's most precise phrase, into Yumpies, young, upwardly mobile, urban professionals.

Leon Gorman faced the problem in the winter of 1983–1984, after spending a year of minimum growth ruminating on the changing nature of the L. L. Bean customer, on the predominance of women, on the trend, all across America, away from hard-core outdoors experiences such as shooting birds and scaling fish. The solution was predictable. Faced with a split market — Preppies and Sports — Leon Gorman split the catalogs. In the spring of 1984, Bean's test-marketed an all-fishing, all-camping, all-outdoors catalog. At the same time everyone on the mailing list got a small book titled "Weekends." Both books were a success, and the pattern was set. In the fall of 1984, there would be an all-shooting, all-hiking, all-outdoors book in which the dominant pattern was camouflage clothing, and the regular Fall catalog would continue to expand into the dressier sports clothing, the upscale household items. The world had gone in two directions, and L. L. Bean was not about to leave a road untaken.

What appears, on the surface, to be a minor reorganization within the company is perhaps the best news for loyal customers, whether Yumpie or Sport. Product managers, for the first time since L. L. Bean himself was designing Duck Hunting Coats (and rubber underwear), are freed from the duties of forecasting sales and establishing inventories. Clothing managers are now charged with designing clothing, not just figuring out how many Maine Hunting Shirts to order. There is a spirit of innovation inside the company at the product level, after 15 years of innovation at the marketing level. There will be new clothing, new underwear, new footwear. Bean's will write specifications for the first time, instead of relying on the old, traditional, "as per sample" method of buying clothing. Things will continue to change, but the buzz word now is *quality* in Freeport, not quantity.

It may very well work. For there is something fundamental about the L. L. Bean customer that has, up until now, not generated much *policy* inside the company. Bean's knows a great deal about how the customer sees himself, about the customer's self-image, about income, education and social status. But the one big thing Bean's knows is how the customer feels about the company.

The overwhelming message from the customer is not that he or she likes the merchandise. It is not that the customer appreciates, or even understands, the pricing policy. The message is that the customer has love for L. L. Bean, has affection that jars the most jaded of customer surveyors. The affection comes from all the component parts, merchandise, price, style, the return policy, the funkiness of the catalog, the State of Maine, but it is seldom expressed in any, or all, of those terms. It is expressed in fantasies, in imagined things, in customers who say, when asked what they think about when they think about L. L. Bean, say they think about a small store, with the lights on in the windows, and the snow falling outside, about a warm, cheerful place. Customers can smell pine trees when they think about L. L. Bean. They use these images because it is harder to tell the truth, which is that they believe that L. L. Bean likes *them*. You may like Ralph Lauren, but I doubt there are 20 women in America who think Ralph Lauren likes *them*. It is not something we expect from merchants.

It is something that Leon Gorman understands, as best you can understand something when you still live in the shadow of the man who created the affection. It is a part of his purpose, as he is fond of writing, to remember that customers have "invested their patronage and goodwill." Whether he is comfortable with the level of that goodwill, something considerably more powerful than mere benign thoughts, is less clear. In return for that goodwill, he promises that the company will "provide the customers with products of value in an efficient, timely and personal manner." One is reminded, looking at that somewhat reticent prose, of the old customer whose letter L. L. Bean himself was so fond of quoting, the **man,** who after waiting months for a pair of boots wrote back that they had finally arrived: "Shoes O:K. Me O:K. Hope you O:K:."

At a minimum, that is one reason to write this book. Whether we should or not, and I cannot imagine a reason why we shouldn't, there are several million of us who hope that L. L. Bean is O.K., too.

BUSINESS SENSE

☐ **BALANCE SHEET BASICS: Financial Management for Nonfinancial Managers by Ronald C. Spurga.** The step-by-step guide every manager can understand, put to instant use, and profit from continually. Written in jargon-free language, with a wealth of fascinating examples and expert insights, this book leads you through a business's balance sheet to total comprehension of how it works, and how you can make it work for you and your company. (625536—$4.50)

☐ **RUNNING YOUR OWN SHOW: Mastering the Basics of Small Business by Richard T. Curtin.** How to find, buy, develop and manage your own business. This book teaches you all the short-term tactics and long-term strategies necessary to make your business grow and prosper.
(624009—$4.50)*

☐ **ENTREPRENEURING: The Ten Commandments for Building a Growth Company by Steven C. Brandt.** The guide that shows you how financial giants begin, and how you too can utilize basic business principles to create the kind of growth-oriented company that will survive and thrive in our ever-changing economy. (621980—$3.95)

☐ **CONCEPT OF THE CORPORATION by Peter F. Drucker. Second revised edition.** An up-to-date edition of the classic study of the organization and management policies of General Motors—the company that has become the model for modern large-scale corporations across the world.
(621972—$3.95)

☐ **STAYING AT THE TOP: The Life of a CEO by Sonny Kleinfield.** Inside the world of Avon Products CEO Hicks Waldron. A business book that will long stand as a uniquely personal and revealing slide of corporate history ... "a fast-paced business thriller."—
The New York Times Book Review (149777—$4.50)

*Prices slightly higher in Canada

**Buy them at your local
bookstore or use coupon
on next page for ordering.**

WINNING STRATEGIES

MENTOR (0451)

FROM THE MENTOR EXECUTIVE LIBRARY

☐ **ENTREPRENEURING IN ESTABLISHED COMPANIES: Managing toward the Year 2000 by Stephen C. Brandt.** No matter how long a company has been established and how large it has grown, it must shed outworn management structures and practices and make fresh use of both people and technology. This is the message of this acclaimed guide that shows how to survive in today's fiercely competitive climate. "Must reading for new and old managers alike!"—William F. Miller, President and CEO, SRI International. (625528—$4.95)

☐ **THE ART OF BEING A BOSS: Inside Intelligence from Top-Level Business Leaders and Young Executives by Robert J. Schoenberg.** Drawing on interviews with over 100 top executives, this unique guide to climbing the executive ladder identifies the attributes that are essential in a good manager. "An antidote to all the recent manuals on how to succeed by using power, intimidation, transactional analysis, etc.... recommended."—Library Journal (623789—$3.95)*

☐ **QUALITY IS FREE by Philip B. Crosby.** The art of making quality certain, and of managing quality so that it becomes a source of business profits. "The executive who spends half a day digesting this book may find it one of the most valuable investments of time he or she has ever made."—Business Week (625854—$4.95)

☐ **QUALITY WITHOUT TEARS by Philip B. Crosby.** The art of hassle-free management. Quality: it's the goal of every business enterprise—yet all too often it's the despair of every executive who tries to foster it. Now, Philip Crosby shows how quality can be produced without twisting arms and with the full support of the executives and the work force alike. "A MUST FOR MANAGERS"—The Orlando Sentinel. (256585—$8.95)

☐ **RUNNING THINGS: The Art of Making Things Happen by Philip Crosby.** Quality in leadership by America's #1 quality expert. Leadership is not a mystical quality, but a down-to-earth attitude and way of doing things that you can easily master whether you're president of a huge corporation or the captain of a softball team. "Philip Crosby is the leading evangelist of quality in the U.S."—Times (259150—$9.95)

*Prices slightly higher in Canada

There's an epidemic with 27 million victims. And no visible symptoms.

It's an epidemic of people who can't read.

Believe it or not, 27 million Americans are functionally illiterate, about one adult in five.

The solution to this problem is you... when you join the fight against illiteracy. So call the Coalition for Literacy at toll-free **1-800-228-8813** and volunteer.

Volunteer Against Illiteracy. The only degree you need is a degree of caring.